BUDDHISM
for PARENTS
ON THE GO

BUDDHISM
for PARENTS
ON THE GO

GEMS TO MINIMISE STRESS

SARAH NAPTHALI

inspired
LIVING

ALLEN&UNWIN

First published in 2010

Inspired Living, an imprint of
Allen & Unwin
83 Alexander Street
Crows Nest NSW 2065
Australia
Phone: (61 2) 8425 0100
Fax: (61 2) 9906 2218
Email: info@allenandunwin.com
Web: www.allenandunwin.com

Cataloguing-in-Publication details are available
from the National Library of Australia
www.librariesaustralia.nla.gov.au

ISBN 978 1 74237 495 6

Internal design by Ellie Exarchos
Set in 10/15 pt Granjon by Bookhouse, Sydney
Printed and bound in Australia by Griffin Press

10 9 8 7 6 5 4 3 2 1

Mixed Sources

Product group from well-managed
forests, and other controlled sources
www.fsc.org Cert no. SGS-COC-005088
© 1996 Forest Stewardship Council

The paper in this book is FSC certified.
FSC promotes environmentally responsible,
socially beneficial and economically viable
management of the world's forests.

To my friend Anna Street
for all your encouragement

and Jenni Sheldon
for your hundreds of volunteer hours at school

CONTENTS

INTRODUCTION

Why should Buddhist teachings only be available to those with some time up their sleeves? Busy parents might feel they need to wait until they have more spare hours before they can start to explore the teachings, but this is not the case. It is possible to practise while you are rushing children out the door, while you sit in traffic, while you perform your errands, supervise homework or deal with colleagues.

You can benefit from the teachings by applying them to any aspect of your life, regardless of the life stage you are at. Daily meditation, ten-day retreats and involvement with a Buddhist group are definitely ideal and perhaps even a longer-term goal for you. Yet there is no need to postpone a practice of mindfulness, compassion, peace and ethics, for you can benefit from these as soon as you choose to.

The Buddha's teachings have been put to the test over the past 2500 years in many diverse countries and cultures. His 'middle way' is recognised by its practitioners as a road out of the stress of any moment into the freedom that comes from letting go of the causes of our self-created suffering.

You may prefer not to read this book in order, but to choose your own pathway. The table of contents can be your guide, as it lists the various forms and sources of stress for busy parents. You should be able to find some of your own there—along with some of the Buddha's timeless wisdom for letting go of the causes of your stress.

ADJUSTING TO NEW SURROUNDINGS

Once I was in a reality TV show. No—really I was. In 2008 I belonged to a soul-music choir and we competed in a show called *Battle of the Choirs*. I found adjusting to the foreign environment and pressure of a television studio profoundly stressful. The days were thirteen hours long. We were learning new songs and 'choralography' (read 'dance steps') and I felt way out of my depth: being one of the least talented members of a choir dominated by music teachers, I was worried about letting them down—on national television.

I decided to observe my reaction to stress, which went something like this: *No! You can't be stressed! You must be calm! Nobody else is ruffled! Be cool and laid-back. You're the only Buddhist here so the least you can do is keep your head.* Clearly, I was blocking my feelings: suppressing, denying and ignoring the stress gripping my body. This was not mindfulness. Rather, I needed to *be with* my feelings of stress, with an attitude of *allowing*. Resistance to the stress was only compounding it. Practising awareness of my bodily reactions and of my thoughts was the most effective way to minimise my panic and a far more compassionate way to treat myself. Accepting my reactions, I settled down (hid in the back row) and we made it as far as the semi-finals.

See also Change

AGEING

Have we not all been trained to be vain? How strongly we all long to feel attractive. We also want to feel healthy and capable of all the physical feats of our youth. What a psychological challenge ageing can be—Westerners hate it. How to cope?

Buddhists know some techniques, but these do seem very counter-intuitive to the Western mind. They include meditating in a graveyard, meditating on the disintegration of the human body before and after death, or repeating the mantra *'birth, ageing, pain and death'*. I admit that most Westerners cannot stomach these techniques, though my friend, the Buddhist teacher Subhana Barzaghi, at the age of nineteen spent 30 days in Nepal meditating on death. (Of 150 Westerners, only 30 completed the retreat.)

What Westerners can do is spend more time contemplating the Buddha's teaching of impermanence, the way nothing lasts. Notice it in nature. Notice it in people. Notice it in objects. Impermanence is the only thing we can count on; change is the only constant. Denial and aversion are mentally unhealthy ways to cope with the advancing years and can only lead to ever-increasing anxiety. Mindful of the certainty of death, we live our lives more thoughtfully as we appreciate each new day, each new moment. Acceptance of impermanence, understanding that we are not excluded from this natural law, is our best hope for ageing calmly.

AGGRAVATION

Funny how sometimes the simplest things can bother us so much. One reason is that rather than seeing something for what it is, we add. We aggravate. Many Buddhists make a habit of asking themselves whenever they feel stressed, *What am I adding?* For example, I am a slave to a tree in our backyard that sheds many leaves, so I often find myself raking. Zen Buddhists would encourage me to see this activity as *just raking*. In my head, however, I add: *This is such a waste of my time*, *This is so repetitive and boring*, *I wish the council would let us remove this tree*, *Why aren't I getting the kids to do this?* In adding all this (and more), I am not being mindful. I miss an opportunity to experience the sensory feast of the present moment: the scratch of the rake, the crunch of the leaves underfoot, the fragrances of nature, the colours of the leaves, the satisfaction of an active body. Zen Buddhists would call the raking 'work practice'—such tasks need not be separate from meditation or other spiritual activities. *Just raking* is potentially an experience of mindfulness in the present moment. This goes equally for *just sweeping*, *just dusting*, *just cooking*, *just wiping* and *just hanging out the washing*. And then there is *just being with our children*, *just watching them* or *just listening*.

See also Exasperation

3

ANGER

In a book called *Momma Zen*, mother and Zen priest Karen Maezen Miller writes: *'I lose it all the time. We all lose it all the time. The point is not that we lose our cool, the point is how quickly we find it again.'* It was a relief for me to read this. My Buddhist practice has not stopped me from losing my cool and as much as I know that guilt is not helpful, I have sometimes surrendered to its pull after yelling at my sons. But Karen is right. We are only human and children can be crazy-making and, at times, so can marriage and everything else.

So the question becomes not *How can I stop losing my cool?* but rather, *How long will I spend in a state of anger?* and, *What is the best way to deal with my anger?* After all, the Buddha said, *'Anger is the single enemy that all the wise ones agree to kill.'* Not that the answer lies in suppressing anger, denying it or acting it out. Rather, treat anger as a temporary visitor (for it is), and as a teacher. Be curious. Try to uncover what you are clinging to: a belief, a vision, a desire, an aversion, a 'should'? Is it realistic? Can you let go? Or hold on less tightly?

See also Impatience, Irritation

4

ANXIETY

It's a funny thing. The older I grow, the more often I feel anxiety. In my youth I was cocky about so many things that I no longer am: catching a plane, walking down a dark street, public speaking, new projects with new clients. Why the change? I suppose when I was younger I lived in denial about my own mortality, whereas by the age of forty it has finally sunk in that I will die and that sickness and old age are highly likely. Now, too, I am a mother and the enormity of the responsibility, the power of my need for my children to be happy, will create anxiety. Whereas in my twenties I could quite easily distract myself from the stress and suffering in the world, now I know better and no longer can.

What is important in my Buddhist practice is that I accept the occasional bout of anxiety for the impermanent state that it is. There is no need to fight it and force myself into an instant false calm. I can allow the anxiety to run its course, be with it, watch its journey and learn from it. The awareness alone will soften the experience. After all, we need to practise tolerance for the whole spectrum of mental states in order to know ourselves deeply and grow in compassion for ourselves and others.

See also Fear, Sleeplessness, Worrying

Approval-seeking

Undeniably, it feels satisfying to receive praise, validation and appreciation. Yet many of us become beggars for approval, constantly needing others to reassure us we are all right. We waste many hours wondering how others perceive us, whether they like us, why they wouldn't. Ironically, those who become obsessed with seeking approval alienate others, for most people cannot help gravitating to the confident rather than the needy or insecure. We cannot afford to allow others—or our perception of what others think of us—to mould our self-image as it leaves us vulnerable. We also need to model self-confidence for the sake of our children, rather than the art of self put-downs.

Inner confidence is far more likely to bring us the sense of connection with others we seek rather than relying overly on externals, such as approval. We can nourish inner peace and self-acceptance through meditation, through challenging our inner chatter, writing in a diary where we become our own best friend, or by carving out some time to delight in quiet solitude from time to time.

See also Rejection

ARGUING WITH CHILDREN

Many of us live with a defiant child. Call them debaters, compulsive negotiators or just rebels, they drain our energy. It is easy for our relationship with a stubborn child to disintegrate into endless bickering. I once listened to a child psychologist addressing a room full of parents and he spoke of the uselessness of engaging in rapid-fire battle with smart-alec children—it is exactly what they enjoy. They thrive on it. They have your full attention and you are being their favourite plaything—covered in interesting buttons to press.

Sometimes we have to think hard and be creative about dealing with problems in ways that don't default to nagging and battling. A clear consequence that they know you are prepared to follow through with helps. A fixed, non-negotiable routine is more effective than coasting along, the child treating every turn as negotiable. Ensuring such children receive affection and positive attention makes them feel secure so they do not misbehave to win attention—I concede though that for some children, too much parental attention is never enough. When muddling through, take the occasional moment to dwell on their numerous positive qualities, which are likely to be their ability with language, their critical thinking skills and their assertiveness—they'll never be a doormat.

See also Exasperation

BAD MOODS

You had an unproductive day at work—your computer was misbehaving, nobody you phoned was available, you made no progress on any of your projects and the traffic home was heavy. But now you're home and it's all over and tomorrow will be a fresh day. Why do you still feel irritable? Why are you yelling at the children and complaining about every irritation? It is because the mind is fast but the body is slow. The tension in your body from a stressful day is yet to dissipate. Your body still feels sluggish, or edgy, and the racing mind can easily invent any number of causes. We tend not to see this. Rather, we fully believe in the seriousness of our complaints and allow small problems to soar out of proportion.

It can help to practise mindfulness of the body. Tune into exactly how your body is feeling in the moment and label it *tired, heavy, achey, hungry, tense*. Don't resist the feeling, or suppress it, but try to accept it without judgement. With full awareness of how our body feels we are less likely to buy into the complaints our mind invents. My eldest son Zac has learnt to do this: often he catches himself complaining about small irritations and adds, 'Sorry, but I'm just really tired today.' Many adults can't do this.

See also Bodily tension, Complaining, Moodiness, Negativity

BEING ROBBED

For those new to Buddhist ways of thinking, this page might feel like a real stretch. A busy parent might find losing property to be the greatest test of their anger management resources. Yet when a thief takes what is yours, rather than feeling angry and vengeful, could you consider feeling sorry for him?

Such a response is for our own sake: anger and revenge fantasies will not bring our stuff back and only leave us feeling disturbed. An alternative is to mentally *give* the object to the thief. I know it might sound crazy but it enables you to let go of a strong source of suffering: feelings of possession. You replace clinging and attachment with generosity. It might take a while to work up to this mental gesture of giving while you mindfully process the shock. What can help is to consider the thief's karma for this action. Suffering awaits him as a consequence of his action and this is cause for compassion; there was probably also a fair share of suffering in his past that led him to commit the theft. Many thieves are slaves to a drug or gambling habit that they genuinely struggle against but feel powerless to stop, despite several attempts. And we never know, maybe one day we will desperately hope that one of our own children can be forgiven.

See also Possessiveness

BETRAYAL

A trusted colleague backstabs you. A friend stops speaking to you. Your partner flirts—or worse. Or your teenager flouts your most basic values. The hurt of betrayal from someone we love or respect is one of the most painful wounds we can bear. While anger or sorrow may be our initial reactions, we eventually realise that these emotions punish ourselves more than the perpetrator.

The best way to relieve our pain—and restore our ability to live in the present rather than the past—is to forgive. This may take time and work and an attempt to deeply understand the perspective of another. It might require us to admit to some responsibility, or remember the times we erred and needed someone to forgive us. It is not about being a pushover for we can still, where necessary, find ways to skilfully defend our values and assert our boundaries. Forgiveness is an act of compassion for yourself as you become free from negative emotions and from the past.

See also Disappointing friends

BLINDNESS

Life can feel so mentally demanding that, rather than acknowledge the complexity of a situation, we blithely accept the first simple explanation that springs to mind. Likewise, rather than see the people we know in all their multiplicity, we label them: they are *the joker*, *the whinger*, *the drama queen*, *the adventurer*. We label our children too: *difficult*, *stubborn*, *high-strung*, *demanding*, *hot-headed*, *gifted*. Such views of our child can crystallise over time, so we stop paying close attention. Yet concretised views of our children can become a prison for them so they no longer feel seen for who they are.

When our children interact with us we need—as often as possible—to pause and ask ourselves, *Who is this?* Look at them with a fresh curiosity that recognises that people change, mature, and behave inconsistently. When time allows, we listen to them with full attention and let them speak without interruption. Rather than shape them into our image of who they should be, a wiser goal is to begin a quest to see them for who they truly are—and to see their 'Buddha nature' or innate goodness. Our children are, above all, ever-unfolding mysteries. We can never fully know them. Same for our partners. As Colombian novelist Gabriel Garcia Màrquez says of his wife of fifty years, he knows her a little less with each passing year.

BODILY TENSION

As often as possible throughout a busy day, it pays to pause and check in with your body to see how it is feeling. You are highly likely to find tension and by focusing on it you can consciously relax it. Bringing your attention to the body at certain points throughout your day is an excellent habit because the body, unlike the mind, is always in the present moment. When feeling stressed and mentally scattered, a few moments spent focusing on how your body feels is highly restorative. I hate to think of the long-term effects on my health if I did not cultivate this habit of regularly releasing any build-up of tension.

Set yourself some triggers, or times dedicated to mindfulness of the body. My triggers are waiting at traffic lights, waiting for my computer to start and chopping vegetables in the kitchen. The ideal time is in meditation where we might do a complete 'body scan', honing in on each part of the body from top to toe. My sons consider it a special treat when I do a guided meditation with them as they lie in bed of a night and I talk them through a body scan meditation. Not only do they sometimes fall asleep, but they learn a relaxation technique that will serve them for life.

See also Bad moods

BOREDOM

There are days when parents look to the heavens and plead, 'There must be more to life than this!' The seemingly repetitive nature of the daily routine wears us down and we find ourselves bored and dissatisfied. One reaction might be to seek ever greater forms of excitement from the world outside us. Yet this can become problematic since nothing outside us can deliver lasting satisfaction. A more sound approach might be to turn inward and see our boredom as a lack of consciousness in our daily life, a diminished ability for subtle appreciations, a loss of curiosity.

We love to travel the world because we reawaken our openness to the present moment, eagerly absorbing our new surroundings with a questioning approach. Yet we do not need to travel to bring this kind of awareness into our lives. Every streetscape, every object—even the most banal—is deeply mysterious and potentially a subject for our wonder and awe. Dare to challenge your perception of the everyday. I like to play the game of pretending I am somebody else, just dropping in on Sarah's life to see what it is like.

See also Unconsciousness

13

BURNOUT

Burnout is when we feel we lack the energy to continue anymore. Under too much pressure for too long, we feel sick, either physically or psychologically. We have neglected our need to unwind, to turn inward and become reacquainted with ourselves. Obsessed with our own productivity we have forgotten to engage in those important activities which don't seem to 'produce' anything: spending time in nature, taking a leisurely dawdle, hanging out with our children or taking our time over a meal where we actually taste our food. Meditation is also an activity that allows us to reconnect to ourselves and tune into our inner wisdom.

After frantically busy periods in our lives, it pays to make time to reflect back. What can we learn from such experiences? How did we cope? Did we achieve what we planned and did it make us happy? How could we do things differently? Given time and space, such questions, and their answers, can arise quite spontaneously. We might even pop in that most Buddhist of questions: *How would I spend the next six months if I knew they were my last?* There is nothing like the prospect of death, the only certainty in life (along with taxes—and housework), to enable us to think clearly about what matters.

See also Fatigue

BUSYNESS

Sometimes we are so overcommitted, so overstretched, that the idea of carving out time for meditation is out of the question. Does this mean our spiritual practice is on hold until we have fewer commitments? It need not. In fact, it is in the busy times that we most need to practise mindfulness and compassion and when practising can most help us. The challenge is to avoid being swept up in forgetfulness of the present. Mindfulness is our translation of the Pali word *sati*, which means *a conscious remembering of the present*. How can we do this during a hectic day?

Firstly, we develop a habit of pausing. A pause takes barely any time and provides an opportunity to return to the breath, the body or even to pay non-judgemental attention to the thoughts streaming through our mind. At several points in our day we have even more than a pause available to us to practise presence: red lights, moments when we reach our destination early, standing in a queue or in an elevator. I call these moments the 'one-minute grab'—spaces in which to release tension and practise presence. Finally, we can establish what some teachers call 'islands of mindfulness', where we might commit to mindfulness every time we: brush our teeth, load the dishwasher, hang a wash, or walk down the hall.

See also Multi-tasking

CARNIVOROUSNESS

Some readers might wonder how I have managed to write three books about Buddhism without so much as mentioning the 'v'-word. I do confess I have been putting it off.

Although most of the world's Buddhists eat meat, many people assume the Buddha's followers are supposed to be vegetarian. After all, one of the Buddha's five precepts was to refrain from killing. My own report card for vegetarianism contains the 'f'-word: Fail. This is not for want of investigating factory farming and other forms of animal suffering. I have spoken at length with vegetarians, visited numerous animal welfare websites and read Peter Singer's *Animal Liberation* from cover to cover.

I blame family life for my poor performance: a carnivorous husband, a son who eats hardly any vegetables—and the difficulty of providing a meal that everyone will eat. To add vegetarianism to the mix would damage my relationships and my sanity. All I can claim is that I have kept a vow I made two years ago to eat no pig products, I bought five chickens to provide our eggs, and I order vegetarian meals when in restaurants. The rest of the time I try to eat meat consciously: acknowledging an animal has suffered and died. I revere my vegetarian friends as highly ethical, unsung heroes: willing to face the truth and act on it. I promise I will join them one day.

CHANGE

The Buddha taught that change is the only certainty we can rely on in this world of transient phenomena. Humans feel extremely uncomfortable with change and go to great lengths to create conditions of security. Driven by fear of insecurity, we enslave ourselves to numerous beliefs about what we need. Yes, we need some money, but do we need to amass a fortune in order to feel secure? Yes, we need friends, but must absolutely everyone have a high opinion of us? Yes, we need some self-confidence, but do we need to put quite so much energy into eliciting positive feedback, approval and signs of success? We end up believing we need ever so much more than we really do. Hence, nothing is more unsettling than change since achieving our numerous desires becomes less certain.

Buddhists strive to cultivate the quality of equanimity, a feeling of peace unaffected by changing conditions. We often describe it as non-attachment. With equanimity, we meet difficulties with patient acceptance and pleasant events without becoming carried away or overexcited. Meditation is the ideal workshop for rehearsing equanimity, which we experience through being aware of our thoughts and beliefs and letting them go when we understand them as a source of suffering. An example: we notice an itch and think, *It's unbearable, it won't go away, why me?*, but with attention the itch becomes mere sensation, impermanent and nothing personal.

See also Adjusting to new surroundings

CHORES FOR CHILDREN

Every family has one: the child who simply cannot accept that they should help around the house. And what a source of stress this can be for a parent. When I ask my eight-year-old to do the slightest morsel of housework, he is incensed. Indignant. Outraged. I am sure he is an intelligent boy but he cannot see any logic in contributing to family chores. When the time comes for a clean-up, there is always a scene. We've tried reasoning, pocket money, contracts—nothing works. It is tempting to join the ranks of the martyrs who give in and say, 'It's easier to do it myself.' But I refuse! The Buddha's First Noble Truth is that there is *dukkha*—that is, suffering, stress and unsatisfactoriness. Our children cannot grow up thinking themselves exempt from the mundane side of life. We mislead them if we teach them that life is only about comfort and fun for yourself.

Now, where did I put my megaphone and whistle?

COMPARTMENTALISING

Ionce heard a renowned Buddhist teacher say in an unguarded moment, 'It's possible to be a great meditator and still be a creep.' I suppose he was referring to those with serious character flaws who make their Buddhist practice a compartment of their lives with no effect on their daily activities. Yet all of us naturally focus most on the teachings when we meditate, when we attend a Buddhist event—or while we are reading a Buddhist book. If our practice stops there, however, we short-change ourselves.

We all harbour areas of our lives that we are not keen to examine. We may for example know some difficult individuals who we deem to be 'special cases' and therefore not worthy of our understanding. Or we may refuse to look deeply when we react unskilfully to toddler tantrums, bad drivers or bickering children, believing any sane person would lose their temper at such unbearable irritations. We cultivate blind spots in our characters. Yet a conscious approach could teach us about what we cling to and what we need to let go of in order to experience freedom. Consider bringing Buddhist teachings into more areas of your life by treating difficulties as areas of practice. For example, each day we might engage in 'calm driving practice', 'children bickering practice' and 'rushing to get ready practice'.

See also Overlooking gifts

COMPLAINING

Sometimes the simplest story can suggest life-changing truths. Popular English monk Ajahn Brahm, who lives in Western Australia, doubles as a Buddhist teacher and stand-up comedian. He likes to tell this story.

'There were two chicken farmers. One entered the chicken coop and proceeded to fill his basket with chicken shit. When he took it into the house, family members asked, "Why did you bring all that stinking stuff in here? You should have left it outside to turn into fertiliser!" The second chicken farmer entered his chicken coop and proceeded to fill his basket with eggs. His family members said, "That's great—now we can make an omelette and even sell some for cash."'

What do you bring into your home? Or as Ajahn Brahm expresses it, *'Are you a shit-collector?'*

He argues it is possible to be a shit-collector not only when we reflect back on our day but also when we consider our partner: remembering and *holding onto* all the past hurts and disappointments. We might feel happier if we let go of all our stinking old complaints and started collecting the eggs.

See also Bad moods, Negativity

CONFLICT

Whether the conflict in your life occurs at work, school or home, relationships can be messy and the resulting conflict stressful. Our words at such times have an effect and if we use them recklessly, we live with the consequences. This is the law of karma: actions—including utterances—have consequences. In times of conflict, thinking before you speak is often the only way to ensure what the Buddha called Skilful Speech—a component of his Noble Eightfold Path out of suffering. Skilful Speech has four qualities: it is truthful, kind, gentle and helpful.

To make Right Speech central in their lives, a large number of Western Buddhists practise non-violent communication as pioneered by American psychologist Marshall Rosenberg, who emphasises the quality of empathy instead of power. So rather than basing our speech on finger-pointing and demands (*'You're a complete slob, now clean up your room!'*) we focus on needs and feelings (*'I feel stressed when I look at your bedroom because I have a need for order'*).

Given that we are all human and family life is so challenging, an indispensable tool for your family's kit will always be the ability to apologise—often. This is the ultimate way to take responsibility and clear the air. I am happy to report that each member of my family of four has at least mastered the art of apology.

See also Confrontation

CONFORMING

Many of us are trapped into thinking our worth comes from our value in the workplace: *I am only as good as my pay packet, or my social status*. We can easily pass this way of thinking on to our children, guiding them in directions that lead to high income and social standing while ignoring what might suit their tastes and abilities—let alone their current age and stage. The need for society's approval leads us to influence their choices—of study, hobbies and how they spend their spare time—in a way that might overlook what our child genuinely needs in order to become who they truly are or, in Zen terms, to realise their true nature.

Deriving all our identity from our job is an extremely limited way to view the self, for we are so much more than our job or our roles. No matter how we see ourselves, the Buddha taught that our self-image is a complete construction, a fabrication of the mind that has little to do with the reality of who we really are. The very least we can do in the work of dismantling our false self-image is to stop seeing ourselves as our earnings or as our position in the workforce. Only then will we stop inflicting such limiting beliefs on our children.

CONFRONTATION

While some of us avoid confrontation at all costs, others swear by it as a way to solve problems. Yet, as we all know, confrontation is dangerous when our heads are hot. The Buddha likened speech to an axe—a tool of precision and power, and a weapon capable of great damage. One invaluable way to avoid the conflict that so often follows confrontation is by writing letters. In my experience, the first draft might sound angry and serve as a valuable catharsis, but through editing I have been able to present a message framed with the Buddhist ideal of Skilful Speech. My dear husband has received several of these epistles over the years and I have always been impressed with how effectively they initiate a constructive discussion. The letter enables me to present my whole case without being interrupted and without the risk of either party digressing. It gives me time to think of exactly the right words to express myself clearly but also sensitively. Marek has time to pause and consider my case—and his response—before he comes back to me. Other parents have recommended letters—or even emails and texts—as a way to keep communication open with a secretive teenager who does not want parents 'in their face'. A parent might text, for example, *I am here to help if you feel like talking*.

See also Conflict

CONFUSION

What should I do? I can't make up my mind! My knee-jerk reaction to the confusion of trying to make a decision is to grab my diary and whack down a 'pros and cons' list to see which column is longer. Sometimes even this does not feel right and I start a process of written inquiry. Making our thoughts and emotions conscious, we might start with a 'mind dump' where we scrawl a string of gripes venting feelings of anger, fear or sadness. Seeing our thoughts on paper, we are in a position to identify self-defeating or unrealistic assumptions: *everyone must like me, I must never fail, my children must never suffer*. Awareness of our assumptions, especially the unhelpful ones, is essential to our personal growth. A university subject I completed had an assessment component requiring us to write a journal about our learning. The tutor awarded marks solely for our ability to identify our assumptions and challenge them.

For me, inquiry usually follows some venting as I ponder questions such as, *Why am I responding this way?, What is stopping me from letting go?, What am I overlooking?, Why am I so hard on myself?* Writing about our thoughts and emotions is a way to turn inward, become our own therapist and deepen our friendship with ourselves.

CONTROL-FREAKERY

Control freaks are widely acknowledged as hard to live with and hard to work with. Moreover, with the universal truth of impermanence, control freaks simply cannot win. Even if they attain some order, a glimpse of perfection, they will not be able to hold onto it and this stresses them out.

The eighth-century Indian sage Shantideva asks, *'Given all the thistles, thorns and rocks, why cover the whole world with leather when you could just wear a pair of sandals?'* In other words, why try to change the whole world when we could just change our minds? Of course, neither job is easy but we will definitely see more progress from our efforts to change our minds than from attempts to stamp out every imperfection from the world around us.

We can shift the focus from *What is wrong with the world?* to *What are my reactions?* From all the different possible responses to a stimulus, why do we choose to be irritated? How often do we even recognise our freedom to choose an alternative response?

See also Discomfort

DEPRESSION

I have been close to several sufferers of depression, and most of my friends have someone in their immediate family who battles with it. Many are high-achievers with an enormous amount to offer the world. The most common treatment for depression these days, apart from medication, is cognitive behavioural therapy, and I have heard more than one psychologist declare that it strikes them as pure Buddhism. After all, cognitive behavioural therapy aims to make us see clearly and realistically by disputing the negative thoughts that depress our mood. It recognises, like the Buddha did, that it is not our situation that makes us feel low, but the way we think about our situation. We may for example think, *Anita rarely speaks to me socially. She clearly dislikes me.* With mindfulness of our thinking we notice this thought, rather than just go on a ride with it. Then we can replace it with more realistic thoughts: *Anita might be shy with people she doesn't know well, Anita might need to speak to others about pressing matters,* or even, *Do I need to feel loved by every single individual in order to feel like a worthwhile person?* To do this process in a journal as a regular discipline is especially powerful. To combat depression many psychologists also recommend adding meditation to the day for its calming effects.

DIETING

We all know diets don't work and that when it comes to healthy eating we need to establish habits for life. The Buddha, the proponent of the middle way, often advised us to be *'moderate in eating'*. Interestingly, the ones who have managed to reform their diet once and for all are those who have experienced a health scare. A diagnosis leading to doctor's orders puts many in a position from where they never look back. Yet we are all dying, and all ageing, so focusing on prevention of health scares makes good sense. I recently read that the decade from forty to fifty is the decade in which we experience the most physical decline. That small fact—and a few too many colds—has been enough to see me completely relinquish all junk food and most sugary treats. Once my body finally arrived at a point of balance after only a few weeks of abstinence, I stopped feeling the strong cravings for sweets that I have experienced all my life. Of course, eating is a highly psychological activity, especially the eating we do when we are already full. At such times we need emotional honesty: *How am I feeling and is food really the best way to deal with these feelings?*

See also Physical neglect

DIFFICULT PEOPLE

Recently I felt obliged to attend a celebration to honour the work of a woman whom I personally find difficult to be around. She tends to divide people: some admire her greatly, others go to lengths to avoid her. Listening to the speeches from a number of admirers I felt confronted. How had I overlooked all these wonderful qualities? Sure, she has some flaws that have alienated some, but I had chosen to freeze my perception of her and see her only in terms of these flaws.

I'm not going to feel guilty and beat myself up, but rather, forgive myself for my mistake and open my heart to her. Next time I see her, I will drop my prejudices from the past and be open to who she is in the moment. We cannot change the people who irritate us, but we can change our own minds. We can acknowledge that our views of others are distorted projections. We can acknowledge that a person is ever so much more than their relationship with us. We can acknowledge the wisdom in always giving people the benefit of the doubt—after all, what is any human being if not an utter mystery?

See also Rigidity

Disappointing friends

As parents, our friendships with others face challenges that never existed before we had children. For a friendship to really flourish all the various children need to be compatible. We also seek friends who share similar values and parenting styles. Sometimes members of one family want to see the other family too often—or too rarely—so we need to find the balance, especially with next-door neighbours. It is not uncommon for a parent to become chronically time-poor, and their friend is left missing their company, even worrying, *What did I do wrong?* Our personal situations continually change, so it is impossible to hold on to exactly the same kind of friendship with someone over a long period.

Practising equanimity, or non-attachment, is key to avoiding the pain of friendships. Non-attachment is about letting go of intense desires for the world to be a certain way. This might mean asking ourselves: *Do I cling to my expectations of how others should behave? Do I hold my friends responsible for my happiness? Do I believe my friends should see the world the same way I do and share my exact priorities? Do I expect everybody to love me all the time?* Often we believe our friends have hurt us, when it is largely our own minds that have made us suffer.

It is still painful to lose closeness with someone we are fond of. Perhaps we can see such periods as opportunities to renew our friendship with ourselves.

See also Betrayal, Rejection

DISCOMFORT

Parenthood brings some less than ideal situations into our lives—situations we could describe as messy, sticky, noisy, unpredictable or plain out-of-control. At some stages, most of the moments in our day are 'not quite the way we would like'. Does this mean we can never relax and feel calm? Our only hope of maintaining our mental health is to foster tolerance. We need to let go of our attachment to stability, control and order and accept that our conditions change constantly. While we can always do our best to improve our situation, it is also important to practise acceptance of *what is*. So we guard against our minds becoming petty, narrow or small and strive for spaciousness. If a drop of poison lands in a cup of water, it is far more dangerous than if it lands in a huge lagoon. Likewise, with a spacious mind, small discomforts become less threatening. Our minds become more spacious when we live in the present, when we practise meditation or when we try to keep our perspective flexible. A powerful Zen saying worth remembering is, *'The whole world is medicine.'* Rather than battling against or fleeing from a discomfort, recognise its potential to teach you tolerance or some other lesson about yourself. After all, our snap judgements are often unrealistic and misleading.

See also Control-freakery

DISCONNECTEDNESS

In our darkest moments, our feelings of separateness from others can leave us feeling isolated, alienated. We can find ourselves waiting to feel loved, accepted or appreciated by others while overlooking our own power to give love, acceptance and appreciation ourselves—let alone *to* ourselves.

Parents are at a distinct advantage in knowing how to love others. As the Buddha explained, *'Even as a mother protects with her life her child, her only child, so with a boundless heart should one cherish all living beings: radiating kindness over the entire world.'* Through the pure, selfless and bottomless love we feel for our child, we understand more about what love is and can transfer this purer kind of love to others. Buddhists cultivate a mind of love through lovingkindness meditation where they wish others to be well and free from suffering. We send feelings of love to ourselves, to someone we love, a neutral person for whom we have no strong feelings and then a person with whom we experience difficulty. Finally we send our well-wishing to larger and larger groups of people, concluding with everyone in the world.

When our hearts are oriented towards love, we grow in self-confidence for we are closer to our natural state, our true nature, our Buddha nature. Focused on loving, we become less self-conscious and more attentive towards everyone we meet.

See also Indifference towards others, Individualism, Insularity, Loneliness, Lovelessness

DISRESPECT

I live in a part of Sydney rich in migrants from Buddhist countries. I meet many through school only to discover they are committed Christians. When the conversation turns to religion, they assume that I too am a Christian, so when I tell them I attend a Buddhist meditation group, they look confused. One Korean father thought I was joking and checked, 'Are you serious?' Many of them came to Christianity out of disillusionment with the institutionalised Buddhism practised in their country—in the same way that many Westerners flock to Buddhism out of disillusionment with institutionalised Christianity.

The mother of one of Zac's friends is a Sri Lankan Catholic with what I consider an intelligent, sophisticated approach to her faith. She made an interesting comment, *'Despite the difficulties reported in the news, in Sri Lanka we are taught from earliest childhood that it is completely unacceptable to denigrate another person's religion. In Australia, we teach our children that they must not persecute anybody over their race or skin colour but I find the disrespect I hear expressed towards Christians—socially, in the playground and in the popular media—really disturbing. There's a blind spot in our values in Australia. People have no idea of their power to hurt others.'*

The words of Australian monk Ajahn Brahm might shake many out of their ignorance: *'When you criticise another's religion, you criticise your own.'*

DISSATISFACTION

Sometimes parents can only see the chores, the responsibilities, the pressures and the problems. Stuck in this mindset, we can lose our ability to be content. We might start craving holidays, affairs, career changes or consumer goods. At times we just need some time for ourselves, and while we can often take measures to inject more joy into our lives, sometimes the real problem is the state of our minds, or a temporary blindness to the riches, both spiritual and material, that we already possess.

The Buddha said, *'The greatest loss is to receive without gratitude.'* While some cultivate gratitude intentionally, for others it comes naturally, but both types can see very clearly how fortunate they are. Their gratitude might arise from being informed about the poor condition in which most of the world's inhabitants live. It might arise out of an understanding that everything we have comes from our environment or from other people and that we are nothing without our interconnectedness to others. Gratitude fuels generosity and increased connectedness to everyone we deal with. It is the fast track to contentment. Why not take a few moments each day to appreciate, unconditionally, the gift of our own precious life?

See also Slavery

Dodgy motives

Acts of kindness can spring from many different motives and I find it an interesting exercise in self-awareness to identify my motives when I am behaving 'kindly'. Over the years I have asked some of those parents who always volunteer why they do it, but they almost always say they don't know—or something equally dismissive. Take the act of coaching or managing our child's sports team. Our motives might include: impressing others with our leadership skills, wanting to do something meaningful to make a difference in the world, proving to ourselves we can rise to the challenge, expressing our love for our child, enjoying a power trip over our younger charges, proving we are a good person or assuaging guilt about a past lack of participation.

Our motivation is likely to come from a mixture of elements, but how revealing it can be to break it down and allocate the percentages (20 per cent because I want to be seen as helpful, 30 per cent because . . .). We needn't worry if some of our true motives turn out to be disappointing (to feel better about myself, to network . . .). Mere awareness of the dodgier motives is often enough to curb their influence. We can also note the effects on our own well-being from helping others: we might feel more connected, purposeful and freed from self-absorption.

See also Self-absorption

DREAD

Most of us fear conflict, and all of us fear humiliation and failure, so any situation where we risk experiencing these fills us with dread. We may be dreading a job interview, a work presentation, a meeting with a teacher about our child's behaviour or a conversation with a family member about problems in relationships. Feeling tense, we can spend many hours leading up to the event imagining all the things that could go wrong or worrying about a worst-case scenario. This is hardly a skilful way to prepare.

The Tibetan practice of visualisation could serve us well, especially as part of a meditation sitting. Using awareness of the breath or body to calm ourselves and create some space in our minds, we then begin to imagine the impending event. We imagine it going smoothly, but most of all we imagine feeling confident, calm and steady. A light smile on our face, and complete relaxation in our body, helps evoke these feelings.

Sure, sabotaging thoughts might rudely interrupt—acknowledge their presence but let them go, refusing to take them seriously. We might send feelings of lovingkindness to the other people in the scenario, wishing them well, and we nourish feelings of love and compassion for ourselves as well. Spend some time sitting with and immersing yourself in the positive feelings.

See also Fear

DRINKING

The Buddha was not big on creating rules for lay practitioners to live by (although he created hundreds for the monastics). He was more interested in whether our actions would cause harm, than in form. That said, he did provide five precepts for his followers to practise: namely to refrain from killing, stealing, sexual misconduct, lying and from consuming intoxicants that cloud the mind. Even so, I know Buddhists (including myself) and Buddhist teachers who are prepared to drink one or two glasses of wine at a social gathering. They have judged for themselves how much harm this can cause or the extent to which their mind becomes clouded.

Perhaps most importantly as parents, we need to model responsible drinking to our children. The Australian government has spent a small fortune advertising this fact in the current climate of alarm over binge drinking among youth. Do we inadvertently send our children the message, for example, that the only way to relax and unwind is with alcohol? Alcohol is a drug that happens to be legal, but for the unfortunate minority who become dependent it carries higher physical risks than withdrawal from many other drugs.

Part of responsible drinking, from a Buddhist viewpoint, is ensuring that we do not use alcohol to hide from, or numb, our emotions. This can only stunt our personal growth.

DRUDGERY

Loading the dishwasher, folding the laundry, putting stuff away—some of us find the repetitive nature of this work tormenting or at best a nuisance. Yet some Buddhists I know claim it doesn't really bother them, and still others that they 'enjoy' it and find it relaxing. Why are exactly the same duties hell for one person and comfort for another? We need to understand what Buddhists call non-judgemental awareness. The parent who finds that housework has a negative effect on their mood is likely to make all kinds of negative judgements that are hardly necessary to performing the job: *unpaid*, *unappreciated*, *time-consuming*, *boring*, *degrading* and so on. Of course, we cannot suppress such judgements if they arise, but with mindfulness we can be aware of them and 'let go' rather than believe them to be true and allow ourselves to become emotionally caught up.

In describing mindfulness the Buddha said, *'One remains established in the observation, free, not caught up in any worldly consideration.'* Without our negative judgements about housework, we can open ourselves to the moment and even enjoy it. We can use it as time to practise mindfulness and to develop a meditative frame of mind where we dwell calmly in the present, undistracted. Imagine the difference to our general mood if we could use all those hours we spend on housekeeping for nourishing ourselves spiritually.

See also Monotony

EGOCENTRISM

Most adults have learnt, sometimes the hard way, that believing yourself to be special—that you're the centre of the universe, and that your needs are more important than anybody else's—is the fast track to having no friends. Buddhism, too, teaches that such a view of yourself is simply wrong.

Yes, every human life is precious, and every child needs to be cherished, but what is special is our interconnectedness, our interdependence. Overinflated egos are liabilities for parents and children alike because they are simply unrealistic—nobody can be great without the help or support of numerous others.

Yet numerous social commentators accuse modern parents of drumming into children's minds that they are special. They cite Generation Y's overconfidence, sense of entitlement, desire for special treatment and tendency to quit when challenged. Of course, there are numerous Gen Y exceptions, but we often witness these tendencies in some of the new entrants to the workforce.

Just as problematic is to provide a barrage of constant praise to our children. Praise is helpful to a point, but needs to be specific and deserved. Logically, we cannot all be special—or gifted—or there would be nobody left to be ordinary. And there is nothing wrong with ordinary, especially if it also means well-adjusted, content and at peace with ourselves. It might even lead to that attractive quality we call humility.

ENTRAPMENT

Often when we feel unhappy with our situation we say we feel trapped. The Buddha might argue that no matter how we feel about our situation, if we are living on automatic pilot, acting purely out of habit, then we are indeed trapped. Yet freedom is available in any moment. With mindfulness, we can always intercept our own karma, break out of habits and go somewhere new.

The Buddha points to the way we spend all day rating what we see as either pleasant, unpleasant or neutral. He urges us to practise mindfulness of our constant rating and to take these judgements less seriously. Our designating of the ratings pleasant, unpleasant or neutral—which we do many times a minute—tends to overlook nuance, subtlety and shades of grey, and moreover we actually *believe* all our ratings and react accordingly. These ratings lead to attachment or clinging: when we see something we deem pleasant we try to hold on to it; when we see something unpleasant, we long to avoid it; when we see something neutral—neither pleasant nor unpleasant—we feel apathy or lethargy.

Since the Buddha taught that attachment is the cause of suffering, it makes sense to pay attention to the rating system behind our patterns of attachment. Taking our ratings less seriously, we free ourselves to let go of attachment—that is, to let go of the causes of suffering and stress.

See also Stuckness

ENVY

I may have mentioned in previous books that my sons are very difficult to put to bed at night. Oh, I did? Several times? I have always felt exceedingly sorry for myself about this matter, especially when they were younger. I have lamented my situation to other parents over the years, and have been incredulous at the number of otherwise sensitive individuals who have uttered these exact words: 'We specially trained our children to go to bed at a reasonable time, otherwise we'd go nuts.' Very helpful. Why didn't I think of that?

I confess to un-Dalai-Lama-like feelings during these conversations. I confess to envy.

The antidote to envy in Buddhism is sympathetic joy—that is, the celebration of the good fortune of others. Of course, it can seem like quite a distance to travel between envy and sympathetic joy. In this case, I need to shift my narrow perspective of the other parents from seeing them merely as 'nasty people whose children go to bed early' to parents who suffer in different ways to me. Humans really do have some significant commonalities, even if we choose to spend our time concentrating on differences. As Buddhist teachers continually remind us: we are all sentient beings who suffer and want to be happy. To transform my envy, I can call on compassion and imagine the ways in which these other parents suffer. For example, they probably have children who . . . wake up early!

EXASPERATION

As much as we love them, our children can leave us livid with frustration. The irrational toddler, the defiant debater, the back-chatting teen—we can see them all as spiritual masters sent to slough away our rough edges and teach us all kinds of lessons about ourselves. It is easy to become stuck in negative views of our 'difficult' child and even to resent them for what they put us through, especially when we feel exhausted. Yet our children ultimately need to feel that we, their parents, believe in them, and see the best in them. Sometimes we need to rediscover the natural compassion we have for them.

Remember that bad behaviour does not occur in a vacuum, but rather springs from what the Buddha called 'causes and conditions'. Is our child hungry, tired or craving attention? Do they feel pressured, misunderstood or worried? Sometimes we need to let our children be children—that is, less mature than an adult, more clumsy, more unpredictable. As we hope people will do for us, we need to give them the benefit of the doubt rather than slapping negative labels on them (*Stubborn! Neurotic! Impossible!*).

To an extent we can even take bad behaviour as a compliment: at least they feel safe enough in the home environment to test out different aspects of their character—rather than suppressing them out of fear.

See also Arguing with children

EXPECTATIONS OF OUR CHILDREN

Sigmund Freud described parental love as *'so moving and at the bottom so childish, it is nothing but the parent's narcissism born again'*. Hopefully he was wrong about most of us. Still, we do need to ensure, especially in today's fiercely competitive culture, that our children perceive our love for them as unconditional: they do not need to achieve anything in order to win our love. As glorious as it feels when our children excel, we undermine their ability to be happy if they feel the pressure of a parent's ego needs.

We all have fixed ideas about what makes a worthwhile person (sporting ability, intelligence, musical ability, popularity, charitable deeds?), but as parents our job is to facilitate the process of allowing our child to become their own person. This is how we practise non-attachment, the letting go of desires, in our parenting.

Buddhist father Piero Ferrucci in his book *The Gifts of Parenting* writes about how his mother's expectations affected him way into adulthood: *'All my mother's expectations have weighed on me, however much she loved me . . . I sometimes have the feeling I am living an existence that is not entirely mine, a life whose course has been decided by someone else.'*

Child psychologists urge us to praise a child for their *efforts* rather than dwelling only on their results. All they can do is their best.

See also Insularity

EXPECTATIONS OF OURSELVES

One little word that can cause us an undue amount of stress is 'should'. We harbour fixed ideas about how others *should* behave, about how our day *should* turn out, about how our lives *should* be, about how we *should* feel and behave. When we cling to a 'should', as when we cling to anything, we suffer or feel dis-ease.

Sometimes our aspirations sound perfectly reasonable: *My children should tidy their room*, *My partner should listen to me*, *I should be more generous*. Yet if we become too insistent, if our preferences become in our minds ultimatums, then our stress levels can only rise.

Interestingly, saying *should* often activates an inner rebel, as in: *I should resist that chocolate*, *I should stop procrastinating*.

My first meditation teacher taught me to bring *gentleness*, *patience* and *persistence* to my sitting, but I think these three qualities are an ideal way to treat ourselves all day long. The mental health of modern parents depends on our ability to let go of high expectations: we cannot live in a perpetually tidy house, nor look fabulous every day, nor achieve perfect results in every area of our lives, nor please everybody all the time. Accept some imperfection as inevitable, and remember the Chinese proverb: *'Tension is who you should be, relaxation is who you are.'*

See also Guilt, Lobotomies, Perfectionism

Extremism

When the Buddha sat down to meditate under the Bodhi tree he had already learnt two lessons: that the luxury and excess of his life as a prince could not bring him happiness, and nor could the life of fasting and physical deprivation. After his enlightenment the Buddha would refer to his teachings as a middle way, a path between extremes.

These days, many around us seek happiness in extreme activities including hedonism, workaholism, alcoholism, perfectionism, materialism, consumerism, narcissism and fundamentalism. All these paths are about attachment or self-centred craving, which the Buddha identified as the cause of suffering. We can see the Buddha's path as one of continually seeking a point of balance in all the issues we face—and adjusting it for changing circumstances. Especially in our parenting. We seek a balance, for example, between overprotecting our children and granting them autonomy; between being too strict and too permissive; between smothering our children with ceaseless attention and ignoring them; between firmness and gentleness. We need to ensure there is balance in our lifestyles or the pace of our lives, and in our expectations of ourselves, our children and other family members. Often we need to protect ourselves from our inner slave-drivers who rob our lives of balance by valuing nothing but goals and to-do lists.

See also Perfectionism

FAILING TO NOTICE

Absorbed in our problems, obsessed by our goals, reliving past conversations and rehearsing future ones, many of us stop noticing our surroundings in the present moment. Yet if I live my whole life in my head, am I not missing my life? At the very least, we could say I am not showing up for it.

One way to re-attune ourselves to our visual surroundings is to practise Zen drawing—and no, you don't have to be artistic to do this: the seeing is more important than the drawing. Sketching an object from our everyday lives—a spoon, a leaf, a toothbrush—is a chance to practise non-judgemental awareness: no need to evaluate your drawing. In fact, we need barely even look at our drawing. This is about a relationship of openness and curiosity towards the object. To draw an object is to dignify it, and declare it worth our attention, relinquishing our usual dismissive attitude to the objects around us. Drawing random objects opens us to the beauty in the ordinary. It is also a meaningful activity to engage in with children, allowing them to practise a deeper way to see.

The especially time-poor may have already skipped to the next page, but if you're still with me yet feel you don't have time to put pencil to paper, you can still adopt a sketcher's eye when you look at your surroundings: notice the angles, the textures, the light, the shapes, the patterns.

FAMILY DRAMA

Drama within your extended family might arise out of a clash with your in-laws, a disagreement with a sibling, or one helluva Christmas lunch. The worst ones are usually about parenting issues but sources of tension can abound when three generations assemble in one noisy room—or even during long-distance interactions. While most of us go to great lengths to avoid conflict, some cannot restrain themselves from dropping anger bombs or making their disapproval clear. It is easy to become swept up in the storm, making judgements, taking sides, feeling wounded, holding grudges.

On the other hand, what better opportunity to work with strong emotions and make strides in our spiritual practice? A popular acronym to help us navigate our way to clarity is RAIN. First, we *recognise* our emotion (anger, sadness, embarrassment, fear . . .). We name it, feel it and be with it. Secondly, we *allow* it to exist. This means we do not surrender to alcohol, the remote control, or our natural propensity to distract, suppress or block the emotion. Thirdly, we *investigate*. How does this emotion feel in our body? What thoughts feed it? What other feelings are present? We do not need to psychoanalyse ourselves, but rather non-judgementally observe what is going on. Finally, we *non-identify*. We acknowledge that this feeling is no representation of who we are: no need to let it consume us whole.

See also Conflict, Confrontation

46

FAMILY HOLIDAYS

You may have developed a pattern over the course of your life of looking forward to your hard-earned holiday getaway as a time for self-indulgence, for pleasing yourself and creating the very best of memories. The average family holiday is a somewhat different deal. In the earliest years of parenting, 'family holiday' is the cruellest of oxymorons—although they do vastly improve as the children grow older. It's just that everyone has a different vision of how the holiday should unfold. Cling too tightly to that vision and you destroy any possibility of enjoying your holiday.

The Buddha's Second Noble Truth is that desire, or craving, is the cause of suffering. When we insist the holiday take a specific shape, we become tense and more likely to engage in conflict in order to defend our mental image of the perfect holiday.

The family holiday is about unpredictability, negotiation and frequent squabbles. The successful family holiday is about compromise, flexibility and letting go. Control freaks need not apply.

See also Control freakery, School holidays

47

FATIGUE

Tired from lack of sleep. Tired from attending to the needs of others. Tired from too much work. From keeping eight different balls in the air. From too much rushing. Parents have no lack of reasons to feel tired, but sometimes we feel utterly drained of every last skerrick of energy: forget being mindful; forget generosity; forget skilful thinking.

Mother and Zen priest Karen Maezen Miller in her book *Momma Zen* provides just the medicine for tired parents with these words: '*A Zen teacher might exhort, "When you're tired, be tired." In other words, don't exaggerate, contemplate, bemoan, or otherwise* involve *yourself with it. Don't reject it; don't despise it. Don't inflate it with meaning or difficulty. Be what you are: be tired.*' Her message is to simply give in to fatigue and notice how it enables you to quieten down, grow still and let go of all struggle.

See also Burnout

FEAR

Potential fears for the average parent? Fear of failure, fear of ageing, of death, of feeling inadequate, of not getting what we want, of losing what we have, of getting what we don't want, that we might suffer in any way, that our children might suffer—to name a few. One way we increase the level of fear in our lives is by believing we need many things in order to survive. We elevate common preferences to unquestionable needs. By telling ourselves we simply must fulfil one hundred different desires, any threat to realising any of those desires evokes fear.

In times of fear, we need to turn inward and ask ourselves, *What do I really need, and what am I fooling myself about needing?* We could also ask ourselves, *Given that happiness comes from within, why am I relying so heavily on external conditions—that are all impermanent—to make me happy?*

The Buddha diagnoses fear as our need to protect our false sense of a consistent, unchanging self. The greatest fear of this constructed self is non-existence, and pursuing the various attachments that feed the ego helps reassure this false self that it exists. We confuse our desires with who we are: *I am this job that I want, I am a good parent whose children never suffer, That house/car is who I am.*

As if.

See also Anxiety, Rejection, Worrying

FEELING MEAN

W e may be in the habit of opening up to those close to us and
'venting' our frustrations about the more difficult characters in
our lives. I know for myself that after such conversations I feel a sense
of dis-ease, even if I experienced at the time the fleeting satisfaction of
purging tensions. I feel as though I have betrayed a higher self. Those
close to us will in most cases take our side, for we have all been raised
to commiserate with rather than enlighten each other. The trouble is
that when our confidants only sympathise with our viewpoint we miss
opportunities to see our 'difficult person' more clearly, let alone our
own role in a difficult relationship.

Some Buddhists make a vow to stop criticising others, and I have
heard them joke in the first few weeks about how little there is to say.

Not that it is wrong to explore and discuss our difficult relationships
with someone we trust and respect. Still, there are skilful ways to do
this: ways that concentrate on the observable facts of the situation and
our own responses and feelings rather than only harsh judgements
of another—even ways that explore the perspective of the difficult
person. We need to be mindful of our intention: do we speak from a
desire to resolve our feelings, or rather from a compulsion to attack
an enemy? *Will this conversation bring me closer to a state of peace—or
does it only fuel my anger?*

See also Hatred, Judging others

FEELING OVERWHELMED

Subhana Barzaghi is a senior Buddhist teacher who encourages us to *break the feeling of stress down into its parts* in order to see it in more precise terms. What we usually refer to as stress, if we look more closely, is in fact a mixture of different emotions. Our 'stress' in any particular situation is likely to have parts of any of a large number of mind states, such as agitation, shock, boredom, panic, frustration, or feelings of helplessness. She then asks us to assign a percentage to each component. One father, Eric, spoke to a group Subhana was leading of the stress of the trains running late so that he could not arrive home in time to say goodnight to his children. Reflecting on the stress he feels while waiting on the train platform, he broke his stress down into 40 per cent *anger* with the government for its inadequate transport system, 30 per cent *remorse* over feelings of failing his children, and 30 per cent *longing* to see them. Applying more precise language to his feelings, Eric feels less overwhelmed. The stress becomes less concrete and Eric is able to observe the fluidity of the different parts: the ways they arise, build, then lessen and pass.

FEELING RESERVED

One way to practise non-attachment in our relationships with those we love is to open our minds to strangers—the man who serves your coffee, the woman who lives across the road, the chatty kid, the postal worker. It is not only those close to us who are precious and valuable, or who can teach us something new.

One Buddhist mother and friend I love to quote is Kim Gold, who wrote in her blog: *'One of the subconscious effects I have noticed since I started meditating is that my spirit has really opened up. I keep meeting incredible people wherever I go and we have these "exchanges". At the park. At the hardware store. At the vet. Yesterday, while getting my hair cut, I suddenly found myself talking to someone and we just connected. Whether it's just a one-time conversation or the beginning of a friendship, we're both left with a positive feeling that I'm sure radiates out to others for the rest of the day. This keeps happening and I love it! I have a hunch that it has something to do with a relaxed spirit of acceptance and openness cultivated during meditation. People tune into this and it makes these beautiful connections possible.'*

Who would have thought that, despite the warnings throughout our childhoods, talking to strangers could make our world a larger and brighter place?

See also Focused on our own

Focused on our own

One way to ensure that our fierce love for our children is not a form of grasping attachment is to open our hearts to other children as well. It is easy for parents to perceive children other than their own purely in terms of their usefulness: a suitable friend for my child or not, a good influence or not, with likable parents or not.

We all know how touching it feels when other adults can recognise what is lovable in our child, so the more we can open to the inner beauty of other children the more hearts we can touch. From my own childhood I remember a small handful of adults who, without being related to me, seemed to really see me and convey warmth—I feel sure they contributed to my self-confidence. So chat to the children who visit for play dates, get to know them and develop a friendly relationship. It takes little effort and helps create a community of loving adults for all our children.

See also Feeling reserved

FORGETTING TO PRACTISE

One challenge for parents in practising Buddhist teachings is to remember. Constantly rushing, refereeing and rule-enforcing, we forget to take our desires and preferences with a grain of salt.

Sometimes we feel frustrated reflecting on how every day we react in the same way (nagging, yelling, ruminating, worrying) even though our reactions seem ineffective and leave us feeling drained. Of course, as a practice deepens over time, we do notice subtle softenings, shifts and openings in our habitual responses to family life. Still, how can we remember to practise when we are caught up in the thick of family life?

One reminder I have found useful is a statue of the Buddha positioned in my backyard and visible from the kitchen—from where I tend to run the evening shift. I have made a practice of bowing to the Buddha statue as often as possible. I do not bow because the Buddha is a king or a God or an object of worship. I bow to express respect and gratitude for the teachings, to recognise my own capacity to 'awaken' in any moment and realise my essential Buddha nature. The bow is a way to pause and reset my inner compass away from automatic pilot and towards a wiser way of living. In fact, the statue is optional: we can bow to the Buddha in our minds at any time of day.

See also Half-hearted Buddhism, Lacking motivation

FUSSY EATERS

Some say, you are what you eat. I've often wished it were that simple: in my case, *I am what Alex eats*. Alex, my eight-year-old, has always been a fussy eater with a passion for junk food. His pickiness has always caused me far more stress than it needs to because I am highly identified with being a mother who feeds her child well. His refusal to eat vegetables and salads feels like my own personal failure as a mother. If he eats a healthy meal, I become a good mother. Just like that.

One of the pitfalls of my identification with Alex's diet is that I can be judgemental of other parents who fill their children's lunch boxes with 'party food'. (It is true that many modern parents are not feeding their children responsibly, but could my reaction possibly help?)

Like many things in life I guess coping with a fussy eater comes down to that old Serenity Prayer: *'May I have the serenity to accept the things I cannot change; the courage to change the things I can; and the wisdom to know the difference.'* A Christian prayer, but highly relevant to Buddhists: when caught up in attachment, let go. As all those early childhood nurses told us, Western children never die from malnutrition.

GUILT—PART I

Mothers in particular live at risk of becoming slaves to guilt. We may feel guilty about losing our cool with the children, arguing with our partner, failing to live up to our standards as a mother, overeating, wasting time . . . the list is endless. If you practise Buddhist teachings you could turn that too into a practice of guilt: I'm not mindful enough, I don't meditate enough, I'm not calm enough, I lack compassion for others. We may also have noticed that we often feel guilty about the same things. Why do we not resolve the guilt-inducing areas of our lives? Could it be that guilt doesn't work and only draws us into a cycle of frustration or even self-loathing? The Dalai Lama finds the idea of self-loathing and low self-esteem—that he has encountered only in the West—difficult to understand. Why would you loathe yourself, he asks.

The Tibetans don't even have a word for guilt—only 'remorse', and this is different. Whereas guilt plays out as a mindless and repetitive attack on our worth as a person, remorse is simply a clear acknowledgement that we have made a mistake, taking full responsibility without taking it quite so personally. With remorse, we forgive ourselves, which makes compassion for ourselves a vital part of the equation. We are also more likely to learn from our mistakes.

See also Expectations of ourselves, Guilt—Part II, Lobotomies

56

GUILT—PART II

I recently attended a talk by American Tibetan Buddhist nun Venerable Thubten Chodron, who changed my way of understanding guilt when she challenged the audience: *'Being stuck in guilt is like saying, I am so powerful that I can make everything go wrong. All by myself, I have the power to destroy my marriage. All by myself, I can ruin a team project.'* She argues that when we feel guilt we exaggerate our own importance. It is an inverted kind of arrogance that overlooks the multiple causes and conditions that lie behind everything that happens.

She continues: *'The challenge is to discern our responsibility in a situation and, if we have erred, to regret and correct it. We have to be able to discern between guilt and regret when they arise in our mind. If we'd put our hand on a hot stovetop and burnt ourselves, we would regret that action, but we wouldn't feel guilty.*

'In our culture we often think that the worse we feel, the more we absolve ourselves from our mistake. We punish ourselves with self-criticism and guilt, thinking it will alleviate the negativity of what we did. We need compassion for ourselves: own our mistakes and harmful actions, purify and correct them, and then use our energy to benefit others.'

'Don't,' gently warns our Venerable sister, *'make your mistakes your identity.'*

See also Expectations of ourselves, Guilt—Part I, Lobotomies

GULLIBILITY

Socially, we might find ourselves believing gossip, rumours or slander because it feels exciting. Too often we believe what we read in the papers or hear in the news, ignoring that journalists often make mistakes or purposely misrepresent situations. As parents, we can find ourselves deferring to 'the experts', when it is ourselves who know our child first-hand.

Fortunately, we live in an age in which critical thinking is part of any true education. I greatly admire the Buddha as a proponent of critical thinking. He told us not to accept anything just because we hear it many times, or because it comes from an impressive source. We need not accept, he continues, what has been widely stated or written in books. We need not accept something purely because it is logical, reasoned or part of a theory. Nor do we accept anything simply because we respect the teacher. Even the words of the Buddha himself we should not necessarily accept without testing them for ourselves. The Buddha concludes this list with the advice, *'Know in yourselves: "These things are wholesome, blameless, commended by the wise, and being adopted and put into effect they lead to welfare and happiness," then you should practise and abide in them . . .'*

Consult your own inner wisdom, your own inner yogi or yogini, to assess what will cause harm. By all means, research a matter first, or discuss it with others, but don't sideline your moral intuition.

See also Lacking confidence

58

HALF-HEARTED
BUDDHISM

Many people interested in Buddhism spend years coming and going from any serious practice. They might escalate their commitment to mindfulness for a week or two after reading an inspiring book, but then become distracted by other bids for their attention. A few months later they might attend a Buddhist event and feel inspired, but soon enough they return to living on automatic pilot. An antidote to all this is to find a *sangha* or Buddhist group. When asked about the importance of friends who practise, the Buddha replied, *'Admirable friends are not half, but the whole of the holy life.'*

The Buddha also suggested we 'go for refuge', or seek protection from stress and suffering, through the three gems: the *Buddha* (who inspires us to awaken), the *dharma* (his teachings), and the *sangha* (the spiritual community). Attending my Buddhist group once a week is the single most effective way I maintain my practice throughout the year. Feeling inspired by the practice of others is a weekly privilege providing the fuel for my mindfulness and compassion.

See also Forgetting to practise

Hard-heartedness

In a materialistic culture based on competition and acquiring material wealth, it is easy to leave our hearts behind. Our culture poses risks to our character as it is easy to become acquisitive, possessive and envious. Interestingly, the Buddha had no qualms with people prospering. Rather, he saw miserliness as a problem. The antidote is generosity.

In Buddhism it is not only the act of giving that is important but the open-hearted attitude behind it. The intention to benefit another is what helps our karma, by conditioning us into a more kind person every time we act generously. The Buddha put great emphasis on generosity as it is an act of 'letting go' of attachments. While being generous with money and giving to charity is one form of generosity, the Buddha taught that there are more. We can also give our time (by for example volunteering), we can give protection or safety (such as not killing household spiders) and we can be generous with our knowledge of Buddhist teachings. One often overlooked form of generosity is listening deeply to others, putting ourselves in their shoes and providing empathy. Another is to give people the benefit of the doubt. Every time you notice a critical thought about someone, try to also defend them. After all, the defence is more likely to be accurate than the criticism.

See also Self-absorption

HATRED

Congratulations if you are reading this page for many will skip it, saying 'not my problem'—few are willing to own hatred. Yet hatred is only a feeling of intense dislike for another, and few can claim themselves free of this rather everyday mind state. Becoming lost in hateful thoughts, of revenge fantasies, re-running in our minds the myriad ways our enemy riles us, is not a skilful way to use our mental space and the more we do it, the more we reinforce the habit.

As with thoughts of greed and delusion, the Buddha suggested five different ways to deal with hateful thoughts, and it is up to us to choose which one best fits our situation in any moment.

One: Dwell on the positive—what are the positive qualities of the hated person?

Two: Consider the results—what is the effect on you of continuing with these hateful thoughts? Tension? A bad mood? The risk of acting on our hatred?

Three: Distract yourself—pay these thoughts no attention and move on to another mental topic.

Four: Consider the alternatives—could you feel compassion for this person? Could you be generous towards them, perhaps offering them the benefit of the doubt?

Five: Use your willpower—be determined; use a meditation sitting to generate a strong intention to resist hatred.

Take your pick.

See also Feeling mean, Judging others

HOMEWORK HELP

In a Buddhist practice, we aim for clarity. What is really going on? For instance, sometimes 'helping' is not what it seems. These days, psychologists are pleading with parents to stop helping their children with their homework. They argue it threatens the child's self-esteem as parents reinforce the message: you are not capable on your own. Zac's school is one of many to send notes home to parents with a plea reminding us that children learn from making mistakes. When the homework is beyond the child's abilities, parents can help in a way that empowers the child without taking over. They can, for example, ask questions so that the child thinks the problem out for themselves. If a child receives a high grade then they can feel the satisfaction of knowing it was their own work.

Of course, sometimes helping children with their homework can be bad for the parent's self-esteem. Recently, Alex had to construct a solar system but only informed me the night before. In great haste, and with a less than cheery attitude, I bunged it together myself. The professional constructions of the other children (read parents) were impressive. At the end of the day, the teacher beckoned Alex and said kindly, 'Congratulations on your solar system, Alex. You're clearly the only child who didn't get any help from his parents.'

See also Homework supervision

HOMEWORK SUPERVISION

Some mother out there has put a curse on me. In *Buddhism for Mothers of Schoolchildren* I casually mentioned how Alex came home from school every Monday and did the whole week of homework in one sitting. Granted, I might have sounded a tad smug. Soon after that book hit the shelves, Alex stopped doing any homework unless I battled him into it.

So what can we do about children who are reluctant to knuckle down? Firstly, we do not take their attitude to homework personally, using it to define our success as a parent or the 'type of family we are and always will be'. We empathise and show we understand that they feel tired and homework is not necessarily pleasant after a long day of school. Most importantly, we try to establish a structure to their afternoon, a time for homework as part of a pattern or routine. Bribery can be an underrated parenting tool, as in, 'If you do your homework, then I'll let you . . .' It's all that works for me.

See also Homework help

HUMILIATION

One day I encouraged Zac to break a school rule. I saw little harm in it and it would certainly make things easier for our family, just this once. I soon ran into the relevant teacher and felt compelled to tell a quick lie to cover up. Unfortunately, he had already confronted Zac, who had told him the truth adding, 'It was Mum's idea.' The teacher glared at me and said, 'I would have expected some level of honesty to be taught in the home.'

For someone—anyone—to see you as an inadequate parent stings painfully. My sense of self under siege, I watched my mind over the coming days indulge in revenge fantasies, honing the perfect one-liner to shoot back at the teacher. From other parents I longed to hear shocking stories about him, as I desperately collected evidence that he was a maniac whose opinion of me I could dismiss.

The Buddha spoke of Eight Worldly Conditions that obsess the world: Gain and Loss, Status and Disgrace, Praise and Censure, Pleasure and Pain. While disgrace dominated in my case, the Buddha challenged us to train ourselves to meet each of these impermanent conditions with equanimity, without clinging to our desires and aversions. I needed to see my situation clearly, take responsibility for my mistakes and stop taking it so personally—disgrace is just another worldly experience. Part of life. Happens to everyone.

See also Shame

ILLNESS

Whether we suffer from the common cold or more serious ailments, sickness makes us suffer. Yet an interesting question at such times is how much of our suffering is self-created. Yes, our body is in pain, but observe the mind and we are likely to see that we add a great deal of suffering that need not be there. We tell ourselves about all the jobs we are not attending to, all the fun we are missing out on, all the people we are disappointing. We feel angry about the enforced rest, refusing to accept sickness as one of the characteristics of existence, asking *Why is this happening to me?* We torment ourselves: *I'll never feel better, this will last forever, and what bad timing . . .*

How much lighter our suffering could be if we could accept that sickness happens—if we could appreciate, at some level, the chance to stop running around and just be quiet and still.

A Buddhist father of two from my own *sangha* years ago resolved to become 'friends' with his cancer, to stop treating it as an enemy to battle against. He argues that this attitude and a strong commitment to meditation has helped him to dodge death five times. His doctors are flabbergasted.

See also Physical pain

IMMORALITY

Most who practise Buddhist teachings were first drawn by the meditation. Some saw it as a way to rebel against their parents' religion. Others felt nostalgia for the hippie sixties, when many Westerners became spiritual seekers or 'dharma bums'. Many wander away from Buddhism when the honeymoon period is over, and I guess one of the reasons is that a serious practice requires 'being good'.

We often describe the Buddha's path as one of 'meditation, ethics and wisdom' so morality is a key concern. Some Buddhists chant a mantra: *'Learn to do good. Cease to do harm. Purify the mind.'*

The Buddha was specific about ethics through the five precepts. These are refraining from: killing, taking what is not given, engaging in sexual misconduct, lying, and consuming intoxicants that cloud the mind. The more positive equivalents to these are: kindness, generosity, contentment, honesty and awareness. The five precepts are not rules for their own sake, but ways for us to begin our own inquiry about how best to avoid harm. (For the record: I kill head lice and dog fleas. I tell white lies. I drink the odd glass of wine.) Interestingly, some teachers take a broad interpretation of the precepts: Vietnamese monk Thich Nhat Hanh sees certain television programs as intoxicants. Winton Higgins, a teacher at my *sangha*, sees compulsive talking as *taking what is not given* (namely, the trapped listener's time).

See also Temptation

IMPATIENCE

You might imagine a Buddhist retreat to be full of kind, gentle, loving meditators. Remember though that the meditators are on a path to enlightenment—they are yet to arrive. Speak to the teachers who run retreats and who conduct private interviews with retreat-goers and they will concede that many interviewees experience intense impatience. They are impatient about the snorers, the noisy latecomers to the meditation hall, the loud breathers, the slow (but ever so mindful) movers in the kitchen holding up everybody else, the careless who occasionally break the Noble Silence. Some are impatient with themselves, wondering why they are not blissed out, why they find it difficult to concentrate, or why they feel sleepy.

The teacher will nod knowingly and tell them that whatever they experience is exactly what they are supposed to experience, and that one of the purposes of meditation is to develop *patience with conditions*. Patience is an oft-highlighted virtue in Buddhism, for it is the opposite of anger. The practice of patience has three parts: remaining calm, accepting unsatisfactoriness, and developing your faith that Buddhist teachings are helpful in difficult situations.

See also Anger

INDIFFERENCE TOWARDS OTHERS

Have you ever been mindful of your thoughts as you walk around the shops and main streets? We pass hundreds of people as we scurry about on our errands. If we check in to see where our mind is, we may find that we are lost in our heads, ignoring our surroundings, or focused on what we plan to do next.

Even if we do notice the people in the street, it is highly likely that we are assessing them in a self-centred way. We see others not as complex and precious human beings, but as *in the way*, *overweight*, *attractive*, *badly dressed*, *ugly*, *cranky*, *walking too slowly*, *dopey*, *slick*, *chic*—just a sample from our judgemental minds.

An easy way to turn our moments in public into good karma is to send strangers lovingkindness, thinking, *May you be well*, or *May you be free from suffering*. I do this often and for selfish reasons: it makes me feel good. I exit the world of self-absorption to feel the warm inner glow of caring for others. So many people in the street look stressed, worried or tired—it is never difficult to feel compassion and mentally wish them well. I especially send compassion to the parents struggling along with their wayward toddlers.

See also Disconnectedness

INDIVIDUALISM

Here in the West we live in a cult of the individual. Our value system prizes independence, privacy, self-reliance, competition and the right to pursue our own goals and desires. While none of these values are necessarily wrong, we can lose sight of ideals such as community, cooperation, sharing and consideration of others. At worst, we can wind up feeling lonely, disconnected and self-absorbed. We easily forget that one of the most effective ways to be happy is through connection with others.

Parents are at least connected to their children and highly concerned for their welfare, yet this is not enough if we wish to fulfil our spiritual potential.

Busy competing, we forget to be kind and generous. Busy mistrusting, we forget to be compassionate and empathic. Busy worrying about ourselves, we make our world a small and limited place.

Interestingly, with our 'self' firmly fixed at the forefront of our minds, we see the causes of whatever happens to us in a distorted way. When we fail, we see it as 'all my fault'. When we succeed, we take full credit. The Buddha taught that there are in fact multiple causes behind every event. It is never completely our fault when we fail—even though we need to take responsibility for our part. When we succeed, a large part is due to the support of others who either help us directly to achieve, or who clothe, feed, shelter and inspire us. We are all interdependent, so we need to be realistic about failures and grateful about successes.

See also Disconnectedness, Insularity, Loneliness, Lovelessness

Ingratitude for others

It is hard to be at peace when you only see what you give to the world without seeing what you take. If you pause to look around the room you currently occupy, you will see reason to be grateful to hundreds of people who helped provide the furniture, the building, the contents, the electricity—others have invested untold amounts of energy to provide you with your current environment. To be human is to be profoundly indebted. As parents, our debt of gratitude multiplies as we consider all the teachers, coaches and health professionals who have helped nurture our children. Those who truly understand this debt find it only natural to be generous to others—they don't even hesitate.

One source of culture shock to a Westerner joining a Buddhist group is that we often bow to each other, especially to teachers. A newcomer might find this jarring: it looks subservient, even demeaning. Yet in the Buddhist context a bow expresses respect and gratitude. To bow is to honour the dignity, humanity and preciousness of another. We can take such a mind state outside its Buddhist context and cultivate 'an attitude of bowing' to everyone we meet—or even practise an inner bow. After all, Indians and Nepalis greet everyone they meet with the word *Namaste!*, which means literally, 'I bow to you'.

INSULARITY

When our children are babies and toddlers, many of us feel a need to take a step back from involvement with the world. We surrender our freedom to leave the house as we feel overwhelmed by thoughts of interrupting sleep schedules, packing nappy bags, fiddling with car seats or the need to chase a wandering toddler wherever we take them. It is so much easier to just stay home. Yet some of us continue in this mode for far longer than we need to as it becomes an unquestioned habit. Living like this for too many years, our children become the centre of our lives, or the extent of our world. We begin to live through them without cultivating any separate interests of our own.

In the extreme cases, children grow up to feel they have to compensate their parents for their life of self-sacrifice. They feel obliged to fulfil the dreams their parents never did. For our children's sake we need to find a range of wholesome sources of pleasure where we interact with people other than immediate family. We need to be open to the whole of life rather than graspingly attached to micro-managed children.

See also Disconnectedness, Expectations of our children,
Individualism, Loneliness, Lovelessness

Irrational jealousy

One day I came upon my firstborn weeping quietly in his bed. He explained, 'I feel so sorry for Yuma.'

A few days earlier, we had added a puppy to our household to keep our needy two-year-old Yuma-dog company.

Yuma hated the new puppy at first sight. She spent the first few days trying to kill her.

I tried to reassure Zac. 'It's like you and Alex. You fight a lot. You compete for your parents' attention but deep down you actually like living together.'

'No we don't,' Zac replied.

Months down the track, the dogs continue to fight for a large part of each day (I think they enjoy it). At least I have hard evidence that jealousy is an animal instinct. What separates humans from animals, however, is our ability to be aware of irrational jealousy and rise above it. To experience feelings of jealousy towards others is natural and normal. Awareness is what stops us from acting on it in ways that cause harm. This means acknowledging the jealous feeling, being with it, observing it, yet not allowing it to define who we feel we are. It's part of being human. Or animal.

See also Envy

IRRITATION

Little things that irritate us in family life are potentially innumerable. This means it is possible to spend large chunks of our life in a state of irritation, reacting to one thing after another. One child whines, the other nags, their bedroom is a mess, the dog next door barks, your partner watches television while you clean up—aargh!

One of the first Buddhist teachings I ever learnt that struck me with its potential to transform my life was this one: *'It is not the source of irritation that hurts you but your aversion to it.'* What causes me to suffer is my insistence that the irritation stop, my belief that it is unbearable and that nobody should have to put up with it. Fighting irritations and refusing to accept what we cannot change about the present moment fuels our tension. Letting go of our beliefs of how the present moment should be and practising acceptance is the road to freedom.

The trick is to insert the pause in our thinking, the moment where we 'stop and realise' we are stuck in our habit of resisting the way things are. Then we surrender, release the tension in our bodies and enjoy our newfound freedom. This is not to say we become passive—if we can make a positive change then we do. We just avoid attachment to the results of such efforts.

See also Anger

JOB SUITABILITY

I recently heard on the radio about a study exploring the possibility of remunerating workers not for their educational level, skills or intelligence but for the amount of good they do for society. It argued hospital cleaners deserve high pay since their work saves countless lives by stopping the spread of disease, whereas advertising executives deserve negative pay for their role in stimulating overconsumption and creating environmental, social and health problems (global warming, debt and obesity for example). Such a system will probably never eventuate but, for me, provides a neat segue into the Buddha's teachings around Right Livelihood, one of the three ethical 'folds' from the Buddha's Noble Eightfold path. The Buddha taught that being ethical was essential to finding freedom from stress and suffering. We need to make sure that in the workplace our dealings with others are honest, kind and respectful. We might also consider the messages we give our children about the meaning of work in our lives. Is it a means for consumption or a way to help others and make a difference?

We need to inquire of ourselves: *Does my work sit comfortably with my values? Is it helping or hindering society? Do I work from a sense of compassion and connection with others? What are my motives in going to work? Do I turn a blind eye to corruption, exploitation or cynicism?* Many Buddhists do find their deepening practice can lead to a career change.

JUDGING OTHERS

If we are not careful, parenting can turn us into highly judgemental characters. Judging other parents harshly allows us to feel superior and to ignore our own short-comings. Sometimes we go through patches where we entertain a stream of critical thoughts about parents, grandparents and non-parents alike. At such times we experience others as so very separate from us, but the Buddha taught that this sense of being separate is an illusion. We enhance this illusion by exaggerating our sense of self, where we see our own self as the very centre of the universe and as a consistent, permanent entity. The Buddha constantly pointed to our interdependence and interconnectedness, claiming no real separation.

One Buddhist technique for dealing with people we find difficult is to repeat the mantra, *'She is me'*. This opens our eyes as to how we have the potential to behave the same way, given the right conditions. We experience all the same emotions as our difficult person. We share the same desire to be happy and avoid suffering. A similar technique after having critical thoughts about a challenging person is to add the words, *'Just like me.'* As Freud taught, so often we are only projecting our own faults and issues—the parts of ourselves we refuse to own—onto another. In other words: it takes one to know one.

The poet Terence of ancient Rome is still widely quoted today in attempts to encourage understanding: *'Nothing human is alien to me.'* Given the right (or wrong) conditions, we are all capable of anything.

See also Feeling mean, Hatred, Limited views of others

LACKING CONFIDENCE

Modern parents are amazed when their own parents tell them there was only really one parenting book in their generation. Today the number of experts giving parenting advice is uncountable. Some argue this points to a crisis in our confidence, that we no longer trust our instincts for we assume the experts know better. Yet who knows our children better than we do? Who knows our personal situation better? And since when is there a right and wrong way to parent that applies to every family?

Interestingly Doctor Spock, the author of the parenting bible of our parents' experience, chooses to start his book thus: *'The most important thing I have to say is that you should not take too literally what is said in this book. Every child is different, every parent is different . . . Remember that you are more familiar with your child's temperament and patterns than I ever could be.'* His first chapter is headed 'Trust yourself', with the subtitle, 'You know more than you think you do.'

His words remind me of the Buddha, who also wants us to trust our own inner wisdom rather than slavishly follow dogma, gurus or accepted wisdom, for he said: *'Know yourselves what things are praised by the wise and lead to benefit and happiness.'* Spiritual practice, especially meditation, leads to increased intimacy with our inner wisdom.

See also Gullibility

LACKING MOTIVATION

I have recently undertaken a short course in psychology, and find it particularly exciting when I discover theorists whose ideas dovetail with Buddhist teachings. One of these is Abraham Maslow, who discussed motivation. He saw humans as falling into two groups. In the first group are all those people who strive to satisfy 'deficiency' needs: they focus on money, security and social belonging, and opt for the safety of the ordinary. The second, much smaller group train their sights on 'growth' needs, such as meaningfulness, knowledge and understanding. They have chosen an extraordinary life and may live to become 'self-actualised'—people who are fulfilling their potential. The self-actualised can rise above self-focus to make significant contributions to the world. They share several characteristics that every Buddhist aspires to. One of them is 'efficiency of perception': the ability to see things as they really are with no self-serving need to distort reality. Another is the tendency to enjoy 'peak experiences', or natural highs. Such highs only last a few minutes but they help people to see the world more positively in the ensuing days.

It can be worth reflecting on what motivates us as we parent our children, as we perform our daily tasks. Security, survival, relieving tension? Or—to use Maslow's terms—personal growth and self-transcendence? We wouldn't want to miss out on the benefits of 'efficiency of perception' or 'peak experiences'.

See also Forgetting to practise, Half-hearted Buddhism

LIMITED VIEWS
OF OTHERS

As members of a parent community it is easy to slip into an overly simplistic way of perceiving other parents. Buddhists blame our tendency for dualistic thinking. This is when we see others in black and white, 'either–or' terms. Parents are either 'working or at home', 'public or private school', 'with sons or with daughters', 'in my clique or not', 'a drinker or a teetotaller', 'a useful contact or a waste of my time', 'blue or white collar', 'local or foreign', 'religious or not'.

Dualistic thinking can see us feeling separate from those 'on the other side', yet this is a misperception. Geneticists inform us that 99.9 per cent of human DNA is the same in everyone. In Buddhism, too, the separation only exists in our minds. Tibetan Buddhists in particular constantly remind us of two commonalities all humans share: we all experience suffering and we all want to be happy. In the case of parents, a third commonality is our collective wish for our children to be happy and free from suffering. To perceive others more clearly we need to open ourselves to nuances, subtleties and complexities, to the shades of grey—and this is only possible if we consciously open our hearts and minds.

See also Judging others

LIVING IN A DREAM

We describe certain children as day-dreamers. We might notice how they often stare into the distance rather than concentrating on the job at hand. While day-dreamers often possess a rich and valuable imagination, we may also worry about them missing out on whatever they are supposed to be learning. Yet to some extent we are all missing out by living in a dream state—the trance of believing the teeming thoughts running through our minds, as though they alone represent the truth.

The risk of living in a dream is that we may never wake up. Or that we may never see the truth—not that we can capture the truth in words. All we can say is that it has something to do with being right here, right now. It is not exotic, nor religious, nor elsewhere.

The dream state is addictive. If we try to meditate on our breath for even a minute—or try to *be with* our children for a length of 'quality time'—we discover our addiction to wandering from *what is*, back to the dream.

The dream state is limiting. We allow our erroneous beliefs and assumptions about ourselves, others and our world to imprison us, denying ourselves a wider, more spacious perspective. As parents, we can teach our children the value of openness, of holding their opinions and views in a loose or flexible way. We can teach them the value of questioning their own assumptions and beliefs.

See also Unconsciousness

LOBOTOMIES

One of my favourite quotations from any Buddhist teacher ever is this one by Zen practitioner Barry Magid, which appeared in the Buddhist magazine *Tricycle*: *'All too often what we call meditation or spirituality is simply incorporated into our obsession with self-criticism and self-improvement. I've encountered many students who have attempted to use meditation to perform a spiritual lobotomy on themselves—trying to excise, once and for all, their anger, their fear, their sexuality.'* Barry Magid sees a paradox in Buddhist practice: the most effective way to transform ourselves is to 'leave ourselves alone'.

Most of us have experienced the inner battles that break out when we try to force ourselves to be a better person, or to feel other than we do. Meditation and spirituality need to be about tolerating the presence of our painful or messy parts so that we can learn more about them. Awareness, not suppression, will help us overcome delusion. So in the times when you loathe the company of your children, just be aware. When your anger towards them feels sanity-threatening, accept it as part of life. It will pass. We avoid becoming attached to some future vision of a new, improved self and focus on observing, and accepting, who we are right now. In a cartoon a monk looks in the mirror saying, *'Every day in every way, I'm becoming a little less attached to self-improvement.'*

See also Expectations of ourselves, Guilt

LONELINESS

Parenthood dramatically changes the nature of our social lives, and often families become more insular. It takes effort to entertain other families or organise social occasions. Modern busyness dictates that many of us go a long time between social interactions—especially in winter. Inevitably we all experience periods of loneliness, and most mothers of babies at some point feel distress over their feelings of isolation.

Intriguingly, the Dalai Lama never feels lonely, and never did. The reason seems to be that he can connect with anyone, not just those close to him. In *The Art of Happiness* he explains, *'I think one factor is that I look at any human being from a more positive angle; I try to look for their positive aspects. This attitude immediately creates a feeling of affinity, a kind of connectedness.'* He believes the key factor is openness to others. Rather than relying on one romantic relationship to fulfil our needs for intimacy, we can open our hearts to many people based on our shared humanity. The Dalai Lama sees the second key factor for connecting as compassion: *'Without the attitude of compassion, if you are feeling closed, irritated, or indifferent, then you can even be approached by your best friend and you just feel uncomfortable.'*

See also Disconnectedness, Individualism,
Insularity, Lovelessness

LOVELESSNESS

With love so fundamental to human happiness, feeling unloved is a painful experience. Mercifully, our children offer us unconditional love and forgiveness, at least throughout their childhood, but we can still feel ourselves to be in deficit. Interestingly, we can love our children—and others generally—more purely if we cultivate an unshakable love for ourselves. As we grew up, one of the greatest insults was to be accused of 'loving yourself'. Women in particular, and Australian women especially, go to great lengths to avoid being seen as someone who loves herself—we put ourselves down and downplay our achievements. Few of us model self-love for our children, and few of us practise it.

Relying too heavily on others to provide the love we need blocks our capacity to give love, for we approach others from a state of need rather than generosity. I find it helps to consider the purity and strength of the love I feel for my children, and ensure that my love for myself is of the same nature: compassionate, forgiving and unconditional. The Buddha said, *'You can search the whole universe and not find a single being more worthy of love than yourself.'*

See also Loneliness

LOW SELF-ESTEEM

Ever noticed how our consumer culture is hell-bent on making us feel dissatisfied with ourselves? If we all accepted ourselves fully and unconditionally, then nobody would buy all the self-enhancing products out there. Women's magazines for example work on the premise that we all need to improve, and they offer no end of advice on looking better, pleasing others and fixing up our busted personalities. The torrent of advertising we endure is in the same business, as are many self-help books. I know parents with stellar careers and high-achieving children who feel a sense of failure merely from being over-stretched, from lacking the time to perform even one of their duties to the best of their abilities.

Zen and Tibetan Buddhists, on the other hand, are at pains to make Westerners understand that we all have Buddha nature. We are already complete, whole and good. Right now. This is our true nature. Sure, we suffer from many delusions and we block our essential Buddha nature in innumerable ways, but if we work on seeing more clearly, we drill a little closer to our core, where we are all Buddhas.

Zen Buddhists claim that in any moment that we are fully present we are already enlightened. Freedom from suffering—awakening—is available to us. So we can put aside our quest to add to ourselves and likewise our quest to kill off the parts we dislike. The world and its empty promises cannot complete us in any way. We need only turn inward to find who we truly are.

See also Shyness

MARITAL TENSION

No, there's nothing quite like marital tension to eat away at your mental health—and living with babies and toddlers is the test of all tests of a marriage. The amount of domestic labour to negotiate, the sleep deprivation, the continual self-sacrifice—it is quite a miracle for a couple to survive all these challenges. It is my personal experience, but also logical, that marital strain eases immeasurably as our children become more independent in the school years; but the quality of your partnership needs to be a life-long priority for both parties.

I have been fascinated to read over the years the advice of more than one 'marriage expert' who argues that a great predictor of the success of a marriage is whether each partner can support each other's dreams. In Buddhism, we call this quality sympathetic joy—the capacity to celebrate another's happiness. In fact, if we cannot do this for a loved one then we cannot claim to truly love them. Love, in Buddhism, is made up of a balance of sympathetic joy (for the good times), compassion (for the bad times), lovingkindness (as often as possible) and equanimity (freedom from clinging, attachment or self-centred craving). It is worth checking whether any of these are weak in our love for our partner, or any other human being we engage with.

MISUNDERSTANDING

Telephone helplines abound these days—for gambling, drinking, drugs, parenting or general problems. The volunteers do not need impressive qualifications, but rather short periods of training—sometimes a weekend workshop, plus a handful of reading to take away. Such volunteers are clearly not experts, so what can they offer? Having trained with a couple of these helplines myself, I know that the volunteers offer their ears. They listen. They can of course refer callers to qualified experts, but their main purpose is to listen with empathy and without judging.

With the helplines I have worked on, volunteers don't fix problems or give advice for they are not trained to do this. Callers—like everybody—need to feel heard and understood. They need their feelings named and acknowledged. It takes humility to listen. The ego strains at the leash wanting to control and direct and generally hold forth. The impetus to tell someone what to do can spring from a genuine desire to help, from compassion, but it can also spring from pride, or feelings of superiority. To truly listen to another person—to draw them out, explore their issue and help them find their own answers—is an act of generosity. It is a great gift we can give our children and others, and sometimes a gift we need to remind a loved one to provide for us.

MONOTONY

How often would you say you feel a little wave of joy rising in your chest? Zen Buddhism teaches that joy is not something we have to search for tirelessly, but rather our natural state. So why don't we feel joyful more often?

Mother and Zen teacher Charlotte Joko Beck explains: *'Joy is exactly what's happening, minus our opinion of it.'* By judging everything we perceive, we block ourselves from pure perception, from wonder and awe at the ordinary. We constantly evaluate, 'What's in this for *me?*', 'How will this affect *me?*', 'Will it inconvenience *me?*', and we unthinkingly trust our answers as though they are unquestionable truths. How can we see clearly when we put so much 'self' in the way? We become so caught in our habitual judging that we forget the possibility of joyfulness altogether.

We also need to be aware of the ways we rob ourselves of joy even when we engage in our favourite hobbies: we might torment ourselves with self-evaluation, compare ourselves to others, insist we perform perfectly or worry that we should be doing something else. One friend stuck a small sign on her bathroom mirror: *'Dare to be joyful.'* She finds this a useful reminder that joy is there for the taking through a simple shift in our consciousness, away from our usual judging, towards pure perceiving.

See also Drudgery

MOODINESS

Nobody wants to describe themselves as moody, yet what are human beings if not containers for many passing emotions? Moods are our internal weather and it is normal for them to change frequently. Of course, not all these moods are pleasant and easy to tolerate. Yet we needn't feel a lesser person if we catch ourselves feeling crabby, grumpy, sulky or otherwise out of sorts. Practising Buddhist teachings is not about suddenly becoming a perpetually calm and smiling person. It's not about being nicey-nice. We can still, however, be skilful about dealing with our moods so that we neither create negative karma, nor hurt others.

Part of being in a bad mood is believing our state is a reflection of some permanent reality (an annoying partner, a perpetually messy house, a stressful job). We don't like to admit at the time that tomorrow—or maybe within minutes—the source of annoyance will strike us differently again. Yet it is soothing at such times to remind ourselves of impermanence, for this gives us a sense of perspective: *'This too will pass.'* Another aspect of being in a bad mood is the stream of negative thoughts flowing through our minds. If we can be aware of this stream, rather than lose ourselves in it, we somehow remove the edge from our darkness. Try it.

See also Bad moods

MULTI-TASKING

The Buddha advised us: *'When seeing, just see. When hearing, just hear. When smelling an odour, just smell it. When tasting, just taste. When experiencing a tactile sensation, just experience it. When sensing a mental object, just sense it. Let things stop right there and insight will function automatically.'* Does it sound like the Buddha was a fan of multi-tasking? Perhaps not.

Of course, there are situations when, short of time, multi-tasking makes sense: we sometimes need to simultaneously feed a baby, stir a pot and instruct an older child. Yet it is more difficult to be mindful when we multi-task, for the human brain cannot think about two things at once. This reminds me of a friend who once boasted, 'I can edit a report and carry on a conversation at the same time.' I didn't believe her. As often as possible, slowing down to undertake an activity with full attention—to taste every bite of our meal, to drive without the radio blaring or to sit down and listen deeply to a child with a story to tell—could drastically reduce our stress levels and help us to live a few moments of our lives more fully.

See also Busyness

NEGATIVITY

We might receive numerous compliments and one insult. What do we focus on? We sail through five green lights without celebrating, yet feel frustrated by the red light. We tell our partner about all the problems we encountered in our day and none of the small mercies. We hold on to past regrets and disappointments, and easily forget or downplay pleasures and achievements.

We 'velcro' the negative and 'teflon' the positive. When it comes to perceiving our world, many of us cultivate a 'negative bias'.

You may have heard of Matthieu Ricard, the French monk who abandoned an impressive career in biology to dedicate himself to Buddhist teachings. Now dubbed by neuroscientists and the media as 'the happiest man in the world', he urges everybody to dispense with negativity and become an optimist. He gives us a hint about how we might transform a negative bias: *'The ultimate optimism lies in understanding that every passing moment is a treasure, in joy as in adversity.'* The reason every passing moment is a treasure is that we will all die. Contemplate this fact and we begin to understand the value in every moment granted to us. Given the law of impermanence, there will never be another moment like this one—it is unique and precious.

See also Bad moods, Complaining,
Overlooking achievements, Postponing happiness

89

OBSESSION

Those who practise mindfulness of their thoughts understand how obsessive the mind can be. Insomniacs, too, complain about the same thoughts circling round and round. Some of us worry obsessively, some of us only think about our to-do list, others desire obsessively: an attractive person, money or material objects. It is all attachment—which the Buddha identified as the cause of our suffering and stress.

This grasping and clinging comes about through our failure to see clearly, and according to the Buddha we misperceive in three ways. In our minds we exaggerate the attractiveness of what we desire and so fail to see its inherent unsatisfactoriness, its imperfection. One charming example from the Buddha is how we fail to see the body of the attractive person for what it really is: sweat, pus, phlegm, spittle, earwax, et cetera. Secondly, we overlook the impermanence of the object of obsession—that it will break or change or simply lose its coolness. Thirdly, we overlook the conditioned or dependent nature of whatever we desire. We tend to see objects as discrete, and independent of their conditions for existing, whereas everything in fact exists as a result of multiple causes and conditions. For example, our obsession with an attractive object is likely the result of *how it appears to our own minds*, which might have little relation to what the object is objectively.

OVEREMPHASISING PARENTING

One evening I dined with some old work friends after an exasperating day of mothering. I allowed myself to indulge in some whining about the trials of mothering my sons. In response, one of the men asked me, 'Are you consistent?' A woman asked, 'Do you set clear boundaries?' While they were probably trying to help me (they didn't), they displayed a widespread assumption: when children misbehave, it is the parents' fault—most likely the mother's. Modern parents can't help absorbing this attitude and feel personally responsible for every offence their children commit. The debate over whether nature (a child's genetic inheritance) or nurture (parenting and the home environment) plays the greater role in making a person has been raging for decades but nature has emerged the winner. Research indicates that identical twins, who share the same genes yet who are separated at birth and raised in different environments, grow into adults who share striking similarities in behaviour, interests and personality. Studies of adopted children have also found the children grow up to resemble their biological parents more than their adoptive parents on significant factors such as intelligence—which scientists believe to be somewhere between fifty to seventy per cent determined by genes. The point is: parenting and the home environment are important but when our children misbehave, or disappoint, parenting is never completely to blame. As the Buddha taught, there are always a number of causes and conditions.

See also Expectations of ourselves, Guilt

OVERLOOKING ACHIEVEMENTS

We all do it. We finally achieve that milestone, but rather than allow ourselves to feel the satisfaction, we move straight on to the next job. We forget to celebrate our successes or dedicate even a few moments to enjoying them. Our 'negative bias' can see us dwell for years on failures, regrets and criticism. I'm not only talking about large achievements like degrees or promotions or our children receiving awards. We also need to feel the satisfaction of small wins, such as resisting a bad habit. The Buddha's Third Noble Truth is *'Suffering can end.'* The fuller translation is *'Suffering can end and this is to be realised.'* In other words, *know* when you have successfully let go of the causes of suffering. Be fully aware in the moment you experience liberation from your conditioning. So, any moment when you manage to shift from blame to compassion, from greed to generosity, from anxiety to trust, from distraction to presence—realise it. Notice how freeing it feels. Lap it up and it is more likely to happen again.

See also Negativity

OVERLOOKING GIFTS

While we love our children fiercely and selflessly, we can also resent the repetitions that parenting brings to our lives: the morning routine for example. Or the evening routine. Yet the path of parenting has so many parallels with a spiritual path.

Both paths require that we pay attention to the needs of the moment. Additionally, children provide a wake-up call about several spiritual truths: that life can never be perfect, that nothing lasts, that the only time is now and that I am not who I always thought I was. My children, too, are no longer who I thought they were.

Both parenting and the spiritual path require of us self-awareness in order to see clearly the effects of our actions. They both require acceptance of mystery, uncertainty, not knowing—and not controlling.

If we commit to being attentive, we notice that our children also raise us. We can even see them as spiritual masters running a rigorous twenty-year retreat. Parenting is part of our spiritual path, not a separate compartment of our lives. For that matter, no aspect of our lives is separate from a Buddhist practice. Our own lives are our best teachers. Pay attention. Make time for reflection.

See also Compartmentalising

OVERPROTECTIVENESS

I was most surprised to read on the front page of my newspaper recently the headline, 'Helicopter parents not doing enough to let children fail', followed by an article about the way overanxious parents deny their children the chance to learn from mistakes and grow into independent, resilient adults. I was surprised because I've read numerous articles and books over the last decade saying exactly this. While this article focused on parents not allowing children to fail in case it affected their fragile self-esteem, other articles talk about parents not allowing their children to suffer the least discomfort or disappointment. (Admittedly, sometimes I wonder if the problem is sometimes overstated in the media and modern parents are simply more engaged and involved with their children's lives than past generations . . .)

When parents are overprotective, they are trying to deny the Buddha's First Noble Truth: *'There is suffering, which is to be understood.'* Stress, discomfort and disappointment are part of life and children need to experience these in order to mature. *Understanding* suffering is not intellectual but comes from first-hand, direct experience. So let your children walk home sometimes instead of driving them, even if they get rained on. Let them experience chores. Don't seek the teacher's head if she reprimands your child once or twice. Let your children have a bad day occasionally.

See also Protecting our children

OVERSTIMULATION

In this technological age, we can easily lose touch with our innermost selves, constantly distracted by mobile phones, email, the internet, iPods and all the other things that go beep. Never alone, always connected, we deny ourselves the nourishment that solitude can bring. The Buddha urged us to cultivate delight in solitude. The quietness of time alone allows us to reacquaint ourselves with who we truly are, with our inner voice, our inner knowing.

In solitude our most urgent questions arise for contemplation: *What really matters? How should I approach this problem? Am I happy with how things are going?* The Buddha emphasised that our own lives are our best teachers, but if we never stop to reflect or mentally process the events of our busy days, we miss opportunities for learning and growth.

Meditation is a chance for solitude, but so is walking alone in nature or enjoying a slow and mindful meal by yourself. Modern parents also need to schedule free time for their children, *away* from technology. This encourages imagination, resourcefulness and physical activity.

See also Too much technology

PARANOIA

'I'm not paranoid, it's just that everyone's against me'—or so some of us believe.

The Buddhist analogy of the empty boat is useful for times when we feel persecuted. Imagine you are rowing your freshly painted boat one morning on a foggy lake. Suddenly another boat emerges from the fog and crashes straight into you. You feel shocked but also angry about the damage to your recent paint job. You rant and bellow at the fool in the other boat until . . . you realise the other boat is empty. Your anger vanishes instantly as it is now pointless. So, too, those who appear to attack us are empty boats. They only react according to their habits and conditioning, not because of who they essentially are. They are not the 'fool', the 'selfish pig' or the 'nasty piece of work' we label them in the moment of our anger. Nobody's character is that set, that enduring or that consistent.

The stranger who lashes out at you is responding to his conditions: the stressful day at work, his aching back, his habit of expressing any anger—or the painful stories in his past. The causes and conditions behind anyone's behaviour are too complex and numerous for a simple label to capture. We need not take an outburst personally, as the attacker, like ourselves, is essentially 'empty' of a permanent, unchanging self.

See also Road rage

PERFECTIONISM

I've never watched the game on television but when I heard that Andre Agassi *hated tennis* I had to find out why. According to his autobiography *Open* there were a few reasons, but one of them was his own perfectionism. His coach, Brad, lectured him on the problem that threatened to end his career prematurely: *'You always try to be perfect and you always fall short . . . Your confidence is shot, and perfectionism is the reason. You try to hit a winner on every ball, when just being steady, consistent, meat and potatoes, would be enough to win ninety per cent of the time . . . When you chase perfection, when you make perfection the ultimate goal, do you know what you're doing? You're chasing something that doesn't exist.'*

Any psychologist will tell you that perfectionists are especially prone to depression. Perfectionists need to work on cultivating unconditional love and acceptance of themselves, and meditation is an excellent place to do this using those Buddhist phrases, *'May I be happy. May I be well. May I be free from suffering.'* Perfectionists also need to make peace with their inner *critic* (read bully, slave-driver) who may give useful advice, but usually in a harsh, critical tone. We cannot be perfect parents. Nor do our children even need us to be. They benefit from living with real people, trying their best—not robots.

See also Expectations of ourselves, Extremism

PHYSICAL NEGLECT

The subjects of nutrition and exercise might strike us as separate from the subject of spiritual practice. Body maintenance might feel like another compartment in our thinking, a separate part of our day. Yet one of the first utterances the Buddha made after becoming enlightened was, *'To keep our body in good health is a duty, otherwise we shall not be able to keep the mind strong and clear.'* His point was that we need to tread a middle way between overindulging and self-deprivation.

On a spiritual path we cannot leave our bodies behind. If we fail to check in with how our bodies feel then we risk eating badly and neglecting the need for exercise and relaxation. Moreover, it is easier to practise spiritual virtues such as generosity, patience, calmness and openness when our bodies feel the lift that exercise and healthy food deliver. Conversely, we have seen how when we neglect our bodies by eating poorly and skipping exercise opportunities we tend to be more impatient, angry and dissatisfied. The Buddha encourages us to examine the causes and conditions behind our actions—and who can deny the enormous influence of how our bodies feel? Exercise somehow grants us perspective on our problems. It is so reliable at providing a shift in our outlook, and always (unless we overdo it) a positive one.

See also Dieting

PHYSICAL PAIN

As soon as we meet a physical source of pain, we tend to turn it into a mental source as well. In the Buddha's words: *'It is as if a man is hit by one arrow, and then by a second arrow; he feels the pain of two arrows.'* We allow pain, or even a degree of tension in the body, to immediately convert to mental pain or tension. While we cannot avoid the first arrow, we can avoid the second. With the close attention of mindfulness we can watch our mind converting physical pain to mental pain and note 'anger' or 'fear' or 'sadness'. We might even notice a whole story that passes through our mind as a result of physical pain (*'Why is this always happening to me? What did I do to deserve this? I've always tried to look after myself. John takes no care of himself and he never gets sick . . . '*).

A Buddhist practice of being with pain is one of being with the bodily sensations and when mental suffering arises, we do not suppress it but note it or label it. This response makes us less likely to engage with the mental pain. Our awareness will, to some degree, dissolve it. Meditation is a time to practise this skill, by sitting with discomfort. As Buddhist teacher Sylvia Boorstein says, *'Pain is inevitable, suffering is optional.'*

See also Illness, Reactivity

POSSESSIVENESS

Modern culture develops in us quite an obsession with what we own. The more we own, the more impressive we feel ourselves to be. Many of today's teenagers, in particular, are intent on sporting the correct brands as badges of who they are and what they stand for. Nothing can deliver us into a dark mood more efficiently than breaking or losing a possession. The Buddhist analysis is that we use our possessions to help us construct our false sense of who we are and this is why losing things feels so painful, as though we have lost a piece of our very selves. According to Buddhist teachings, the cause of human suffering is our preoccupation with *'I, me and mine'*, where we see our possessions as colonies or outposts of the self. The Buddha advised us to meet every object, every phenomenon, every experience with the words, *'This is not mine. I am not this. This is not my self'*, as a way to avoid our habit of using what is outside us to define ourselves.

Besides, in a world of impermanence, we cannot truly own anything, for all possession is fleeting. It is also worth remembering that our children do not belong to us, or in the words of the poet Khalil Gibran, *'you are the bows from which your children as living arrows are sent forth'*.

See also Being robbed

POSTPONING HAPPINESS

I call it 'I'll be happy when' syndrome: *I'll be happy when the house is clean. I'll be happy when I've finished all my work. I'll be happy when my partner changes that behaviour.* Or when the kids move out. When happiness is always around the corner, we can never be happy now—which means we can never be happy. Some of us are perfectly capable of celebrating achievements, but deny ourselves any enjoyment from the long, winding process on the way to the achievements. Or we divide our day into pleasant tasks ('me time') and unpleasant tasks (errands, administration, general slavery), lamenting how the overwhelming majority of our tasks are unpleasant.

Why not simply choose to be happy more of the time? To enjoy more of our daily activities? It is not compulsory to frown as we scurry to the post office and the bank. We do not have to resent housework. It is quite possible to relax as we drive our cars. A gesture I find helpful throughout the day and that reminds me of the possibility of enjoying myself is to smile. The Buddha himself wears a smile of serenity if we consider his face on the ubiquitous statues. It is an easy experiment to test for yourself: do you feel subtly happier when you smile? I always find I do.

See also Negativity

PROCRASTINATION

Remember the days of cramming for exams, or leaving work projects until the last minute and losing sleep to meet the deadline?

I don't.

While all of the other 136 problems I list in this book come straight from my own personality, I've never been a procrastinator. My dread of pressure and stress in fact sees me delivering work well before a deadline. But before you start hating me I can admit that when it comes to household problems—leaks, drips, repairs, entire renovation jobs—I am very slow to pick up the phone (drives my husband nuts!). I feel so out of my depth and open to exploitation when talking to tradesmen about construction issues. So I do understand that the problem of procrastination is one of seeing clearly. A procrastinator exaggerates the unpleasantness of a task. They overestimate how long it will take and underestimate their ability to perform. They imagine experiencing only negative emotions. They might focus on the potential to fail, or they might worry about delivering something less than perfect. My mother's words to any of her children groaning about some looming task were always, 'Just start. Once you get going, it's never as bad as you thought it would be.' She was usually right. Procrastination is about living in an unpleasant future, when you could be using the present moment.

PROTECTING OUR CHILDREN

While modern parents have many fears for their children, some of the main ones are that their children might suffer drug or alcohol addiction, sexual exploitation, or peer group pressure to behave recklessly. The best insurance against any of these disasters is to keep communication lines open with our children. For our children to see us as approachable confidants they need to trust that we will not become hysterical, alarmist or overbearing when they raise heavy topics. We might even need to fake some calmness, hide our anxiety or practise restraint for the sake of open communication.

In 2007, the Australian government distributed a publication to every home entitled *Talking with Your Kids about Drugs*, underlining the important role parents can play in prevention. A quotation: *'One of the most effective deterrents to drug use amongst young people is a parent who is devoted to spending time with them. Someone who talks with them about their friends, what goes on at school, the sport they play, what interests them.'*

In other words, be present and attentive for your children. Of course, even the best parents, through no fault of their own, may endure drug dependency in their child, but all we can do is our best. On all the social issues facing our children, being informed is added protection so we can separate the numerous myths from the facts.

See also Overprotectiveness

PUTTING OURSELVES DOWN

This page is for mothers. Although we were raised in an era of unprecedented respect for females, the way we talk about ourselves socially sounds like we are competing for last place. While self-deprecating humour can be charming, women can take it too far, habitually referring to themselves as disorganised, slack, bumbling, incompetent and out of control. Many of us downplay our contributions, achievements and importance. Humility is a beautiful quality, but we need to find a middle road between publicly bullying ourselves and self-promotion. Is all this a hangover from our youth when, surrounded by insecure friends, we avoided standing out? Do we do it to avoid disapproval from others? Our daughters in particular need us to model self-confidence and self-respect so they can see these as possible and as socially acceptable. We can ask ourselves a simple question next time we catch ourselves at it: *Would I feel comfortable talking like this about anybody else, or would it seem too critical?*

REACTIVITY

We tend to live reactively, responding unquestioningly to our every impulse. We feel sad so we eat. We feel bored, so we switch on the television or go shopping. We feel angry with our children so we lash out. We feel stressed, so we work harder. The trouble is that living so impulsively we lose sight of our choices in any moment. Every thought, every impulse, becomes our master, we the slave. We lose the ability to choose our reactions and we become creatures of habit. At worst, we become automatons, sleepwalking through our lives.

Meditation is a chance to study our impulsiveness. The instructions are usually to sit without responding to every ache, every itch. We sit with the ache. We sit with the itch. We sit with the impulse to shift our sore leg, to scratch the itch, and we observe the reaction in our mind. We see the tendency for a mental reaction in response to physical pain. We might see our tendency to catastrophise (*This pain will get worse and worse!*), to grow angry, to surrender to self-pity. We might also see that the pain or itch is impermanent, that it is made up of several different types of sensations. These days, however, many Buddhist teachers discourage us from enduring extreme discomfort as this is hardly compassionate to ourselves and can even set up unhealthy authoritarian relationships among our inner 'selves'.

See also Physical pain

REJECTION

The pain of rejection can torment us for many years. The lover who broke it off with us, the friend who cut contact, the group that excluded us or the string of employers who did not give us a job after all those interviews—it takes great resilience to bounce back. At such times, the sense of the self is at its strongest. We have an exaggerated sense of a 'me' that is separate, isolated and deeply wounded. Yet the Buddha taught that it is this sense of a self—permanent, enduring and consistent—that is at the root of our suffering.

It is not that we do not exist. Buddhism is not nihilism. We just do not exist in anything like the way we think we do. Our so-called self-image is really just a prison: it limits us and stops us from fulfilling our potential, or realising our true nature. We can't afford to define ourselves by our experiences of rejection. Doing this allows others to dictate our worth. We are so much more than another's opinion of us. Often it is a simple matter of finding our niche, our home. Many look back on their rejections with relief, seeing with hindsight that something better was waiting for them.

It can feel especially painful to watch our child experience rejection. A degree of protection comes from ensuring they have several sources of self-worth.

See also Approval-seeking, Disappointing friends,
Fear, Unemployment

RESISTANCE

Often dubbed the best-selling self-help book of all time, M. Scott Peck's *The Road Less Travelled* starts thus: *'Life is difficult. This is a great truth, one of the greatest truths.* It is a great truth because once we truly see this truth, we transcend it.'* The asterisk directs the reader to the bottom of the page where he acknowledges his source as the Buddha's First Noble Truth. If we can expect and accept difficulty, inconvenience, imperfection and all life's unrelenting unsatisfactoriness, then we might be able to calm down.

I learnt this truth through home renovation. Renovation jobs are highly likely to go wrong, take ages and cost more than planned. The result is sometimes not what you expected and, once finally completed . . . something goes askew. Imagine the state of your mental health if you allowed all of this to surprise you. Same in life: there are computer viruses, blocked toilets, office politics, disappointments.

A Buddhist extremist might welcome it all as a chance to practise patience. The rest of us can learn to avoid hitching our happiness to external conditions quite so much; that is, we learn to gradually increase our acceptance. A sense of perspective helps: most of these annoyances we forget about in no time. Also, making our spiritual life a priority provides an incentive to rise above petty difficulties.

RIGIDITY

Human beings are very uncomfortable with uncertainty, with mystery, with not knowing.

Throughout human history, just as in our own lives, we have been only too happy to invent an answer, or a theory, rather than accept some mystery. So we jump to conclusions, believe we can read people's minds and believe most of the random thoughts that pop into our heads—rather than admit we do not know.

As parents, we pressure ourselves to know everything, to know what to do and say in every situation, to instantly solve our children's problems. Yet a Buddhist practice is about opening ourselves to the mystery around us and admitting to not knowing. With this approach, we become more open, more curious, more engaged—and more alive. We are less likely to bore our children with preaching, or the same old answers, the same old lectures. We listen to them more and we listen deeply, not distractedly, so our children are more likely to feel heard and understood. The Buddha warned against rigidity, or 'attachment' to our views: *'It is not proper for a wise man . . . to come to the conclusion: this alone is Truth, and everything else is false.'* Holding tightly to our views, and using them to reinforce our idea of who we are, we effectively construct a prison for ourselves. The only escape is to surrender to mystery, to embrace not knowing.

See also Difficult people

ROAD RAGE

Parents spend hours a week on the road commuting to work, playing taxi-driver for their children or even driving somewhere for a hard-earned break. Few of us have been spared an encounter with a road-rager, the driver who swears, rants or makes rude gestures—often with very little provocation. Our reaction tends to be a bitter mixture of shock and indignation. We instantly consider revenge—answering back or beeping our horn—but usually think better of it. They might be dangerous. We recount the episode to friends and family and generally take a fair while to put it behind us. Most of all, we hope the rager receives some kind of comeuppance.

Attempting to apply Buddhist teachings to such occasions I remind myself that the rager must suffer from numerous relationship problems to be behaving like this. The bad behaviour does not occur in a vacuum, but is the result of past karma and also sows the seeds for future karma—none of it promising. Acknowledging the suffering in the life of the rager helps us to cool down—and this is helpful for our own karma as we avoid becoming a reactive hot-head. If this is difficult, imagine him as your child. Of course, we also need as we drive to take responsibility for our own behaviour—and language—especially with children in the back listening.

See also Paranoia

109

SCHOOL HOLIDAYS

Tick any boxes that capture your role during your average week at home on a school holiday:

- ☐ taxi-driver
- ☐ social secretary
- ☐ recreation officer
- ☐ events manager
- ☐ fun planner.

While we might allow modern technology to 'babysit' the children and provide us with the odd break from these roles, many parents run themselves ragged to avoid hearing those guilt-inducing words: 'I'm bored.' In the darkest recesses of our mind, we might vaguely remember a time when childhood wasn't quite so busy, quite so structured, planned and non-stop-stimulating. We might remember our own childhoods and how we sometimes experienced boredom. We may also recall how boredom could be the precondition for new games, wild ideas, physical activity, creativity or exciting adventures. Never allowed to be bored, our children are less free to grow into their true selves for they have no time to discover or pursue their natural interests.

Every school holiday, I try to allow regular time for the boys to be screen-free, with nothing planned. Sometimes they complain for a while, but I am invariably impressed with their ability to invent a wholesome activity to fill the vacuum.

See also Family holidays, Stuckness

SEARCHING

For most of my life I expected to find happiness from big, splashy events: a financial windfall, winning a competition, finding the perfect job, a romance, some recognition, an overseas trip. As I grew older I learnt that such events were not the most reliable sources of happiness for me, especially not any kind of lasting happiness. I was often surprised to experience a sense of anti-climax at the arrival of such events, or sometimes nothing more than immense relief that a strong craving was finally satisfied.

For me, the best lesson about growing older has been my increased understanding that contentment is something I cultivate within myself and for which I need not rely on external circumstances—which are unreliable and will always change. Becoming happy is about learning to look deeply into the faces of my children, learning to enjoy my walk to the post office, and knowing when to pause and absorb the beauty of any moment. When I am able to find the joy in simple tasks, I condition my mind into one that is more calm and content. Nourishing my inner life—through meditation, awareness of the present moment, and cultivating compassion for myself and others—is a far safer bet on happiness than trying to control my external conditions.

See also Seeking freedom

SEEKING FREEDOM

The monk Ajahn Brahm is a walking treasury of illuminating anecdotes. Here is one I heard him tell at the Buddhist Mitra Conference:

'Five children play a wishing game. Whoever expresses the superior wish wins. The first child says, "I wish for the latest video game." The second child is smarter: "I wish for a whole video game store." Child number three is quite the visionary: "I wish for one billion dollars US, then I can buy the videogame store and my school. That way when Mum says do your homework and stop playing the video game I can tell her I own the school and I've directed them to give me no homework." The fourth child is smarter still: "My wish is for three more wishes: then I could buy the video store, get a billion dollars—and another three wishes." The fifth child says, "I wish I was so content that I never needed any more wishes."'

Child number five won. As Ajahn Brahm explains, the fourth child wished for freedom *of* desires whereas the fifth child wished for freedom *from* desires. Our society promotes freedom *of* desires, yet this will not bring us the freedom we seek, for it will remain impossible to satisfy our inexhaustible cravings. Freedom *from* desire is true freedom. Practise turning inward to find contentment rather than always relying on your external conditions.

See also Searching

SELF-ABSORPTION

Every now and then we can feel taken aback by our own self-absorption, thinking *I've thought about nobody but myself for too many hours/days/weeks*. For parents there is a quick escape from this kind of guilt: along with training our attention back on our children, there is always volunteering. No matter what time of the year, our communities are always seeking free parent labour. Volunteering is letting go of our attachment to time: our need to use it efficiently and hoard it for our own goals.

Of course, parents can volunteer with all sorts of motives: to assuage guilt, to be seen as helping, to appease children who want us around, or to make new friends. If, however, we want our volunteering to create good karma for ourselves, then we need to ensure our motives include generosity or a genuine desire to benefit others. Karma works through creating habits that condition us into a certain type of person. Every generous act—or more importantly, the open-hearted intention behind the act—contributes to a habit that gradually shapes us into a kinder person. We can ensure our motives are wholesome by focusing on how our volunteering contributes to the happiness of others, how we ease their suffering and stress. We might for example say in our minds as we help another, *May you be well*.

See also Dodgy motives, Hard-heartedness, Shyness

SELF-CRITICISM

Have you ever made new year's resolutions? Or do you ever find yourself starting sentences, *From now on, I'm going to be more . . .* We may have wanted to be a more disciplined dieter, a better parent, a nicer person—and assumed we could achieve these goals through sheer 'striving' and 'willing'. A Buddhist approach to self-transformation is to focus not so much on how inadequate we are and how much we need to improve, but on non-judgemental awareness of our thoughts and feelings. Our behaviour springs from causes, and we need to see some of these causes clearly before we can take responsibility for them. After all, how can we change what we cannot even see?

With this approach, the problem is not so much 'wrong' thoughts but unacknowledged thoughts—those thoughts we do not get around to noticing. So practise mindfulness of your thoughts by being more aware of the chatter passing through your head. It is often difficult in the rush of life to be mindful of our thoughts as they are happening. I have learnt throughout my day to pause and 'hit the rewind button' by asking myself, *Where have my thoughts wandered to in the last couple of minutes?* Not that you have to stop and psychoanalyse yourself. Awareness by itself is enough to learn more about the role of thoughts in your life.

See also Self-doubt

SELF-DOUBT

Practising Buddhist teachings leads to an increased intimacy with your own inner chatter. Believe me, this can be humbling. Over the years I have had cause to say to myself: *I can't believe my own narcissism/obsessiveness/paranoia/self-absorption/bitchiness*—et cetera. It is enough to make you stop watching your thoughts altogether. Fortunately, when you are part of a Buddhist community, you quickly learn that you are no special case and that everybody else is just as horrified by the contents of their minds as you are.

In Buddhism, the antidote to self-doubt is—believe it or not—faith. Many flinch at this word, thinking it requires blind obedience to scripture, gurus or something they cannot even perceive with their senses. In Buddhism, faith comes from reasoning and from observation of our experience. It is faith in our own capacity to practise the teachings, and faith in how much the teachings can help us. Buddhists describe faith as 'going for refuge' in the three jewels: the *Buddha* (faith in the possibility of waking up from delusion as the Buddha did), the *dharma* (the Buddha's teachings) and the *sangha* (the community of *dharma* practitioners). Faith is therefore finding protection from the stress of life in these three jewels—and as a refuge from modern life they sure beat consumerism, perfectionism, hedonism, fundamentalism, alcoholism or any of the other -isms on offer.

See also Self-criticism

SERIOUSNESS

In the most disabling phases of parenting—such as those involving sleep deprivation, tantrum-management, or incessant sibling bickering—a great risk is that we lose our sense of humour. After all, if we had one of our closest friends beside us we could probably find ourselves laughing at the absurdity of it all. Why not transfer the humorous outlook we enjoy with close friends to more parenting scenarios? Buddhist scriptures reveal that the Buddha engaged in quipping and was never above some witty repartee. The Dalai Lama loves a good giggle and seems wide open to the humour of a situation. Living in the present moment leaves us more appreciative of the absurd, of spontaneity, playfulness and fun.

One of the greatest blessings of children is their taste for these qualities. They remind us of the long-forgotten joys of tickling, rumbling, pulling faces, speaking in funny voices and being ridiculous. We let go of our very important self with its attachment to effective time management and come a little closer to who we truly are. Children allow us to act in ways we wouldn't dream of in adult company and put us back in touch with long-lost parts of ourselves. If we let them.

SHAME

Perhaps you don't believe in smacking, yet you've just slapped your child. Or you've shrieked at your children in a way that sounded a tad hysterical. Utterly frustrated, you feel shame and self-disgust at your behaviour. Take heart, there is no need to wallow in this wretched space for long.

At this point we can always pause and bring our attention to our body in the present moment.

Noticing the tension, the shallow breathing and our own aversion to our current feelings, we broaden our perspective to one large enough to include some compassion for self. Dwell in the present moment, in all its unsatisfactoriness, resisting nothing, making no judgements. From this gentler place we allow ourselves some curiosity about what happened and some openness to the lessons on offer. *What were the causes and conditions leading to my outburst? Fatigue, pressure, fear, old stories about myself? What am I clinging to? And what possible causes of suffering could I let go of?*

Don't bother trying to somehow kill off your perceived flaws right there and then; the aim is for clear seeing. Always forgive yourself. No matter how many times you fall.

See also Humiliation

117

SHYNESS

For most of us, there's nothing quite as anxiety-inducing as walking into a room full of strangers, or half-strangers, obliged to socialise. Our first question when facing a social gathering is usually 'Who's going?' Often we walk in with an agenda: *Find interesting or familiar people, avoid strangers or misfits*. Our agenda becomes a habitual approach to socialising which we forget to question. Yet caught up in our own discomfort, painfully self-conscious, we forget that we are not the only person in the room feeling this way.

Gatherings tend to settle into cliques, and if you don't belong to one you can only hope for someone sensitive enough to notice and include you. Such people are the social treasures, attuned to the needs of others and empowered by the knowledge that they can put people at ease. This can take a measure of both self-confidence and energy, and we are all at a different point on the introvert–extrovert spectrum—even if that point varies with changing conditions. For the sake of others—and our own karma—sensitivity and openness might be a superior agenda for social occasions.

See also Low self-esteem, Self-absorption

SIBLING SQUABBLES

Fighting between children is, for many, the most trying aspect of parenting. There is one foolproof way to avoid it: have only one child.

Parenting literature on this topic can hardly help us, for bickering is an inevitable part of childhood for brothers and sisters. The only useful advice I have ever read on the subject instructs parents to avoid becoming involved: the argument goes that the bickering only escalates when a refereeing-parent is around to make judgements, take sides and increase the drama. This approach can work to a point, yet at my house, if I do not intervene, violence can erupt: *'Of course I had to hit him if you're not going to stop him!'*

My own solace comes from talking to parents of only children who worry about the effects of their child 'never battling' with a sibling. Such parents need to find ways to ensure their children have opportunities to learn about resolving conflict, allowing conflict to blow over, compromising, losing at games and experiencing the uglier depths of human interaction.

Meanwhile, we can focus on working with our reactions. On a good day, we might even embrace the opportunity to practise patience or recognise the humour in the absurdity of most arguments between children.

See also Compartmentalising, Seriousness

SLAVERY

A boy runs up to his mother in the park, 'Could you put my bike in the car and get my skateboard—and I'm hungry too.' The mother rolls her eyes and replies, 'How about saying please!' adding, 'What did your last slave die of?'

I too can feel like a slave. My eight-year-old in particular seems to require far more than two parents: he needs one to prepare his meals and snacks, one to pick up after him, one to play games with him, one to 'watch me Mum' and one to argue with him all day about who should be doing what. The late-afternoon shift of homework supervision, dinner preparation and household tasks sometimes makes even the most patient among us feel trapped in a life of slavery to the needs of others.

I find it helpful at such times to remember all the mothers separated from their children: the maids working in countries such as Hong Kong and Dubai who cannot even be in the same country as their children. A South African once told me of his childhood maid's descent into alcoholism, fuelled by the pain of separation from her children. Even in our own country, countless mothers yearn to be with their children right now but for economic reasons cannot always be with them as much as they want to be.

See also Dissatisfaction

Sleep deprivation

It comes as no surprise to parents that sleep deprivation, according to the United Nations, is an effective form of torture. It seems so cruel that nature singles out a proportion of parents to suffer so dreadfully. When sleep deprived, we discover how petty, mean, short-tempered and cranky we can be. We may discover a potential to treat even those we love in a way that appals us. Yet it is so very crucial to avoid judging ourselves harshly for the discoveries we make about our dark side. We need to be patient and compassionate with ourselves, for if we are not the price can be high: we can descend into self-loathing, cynicism or full-blown depression. We risk losing our sense of humour or our capacity to shift our perspective.

A crucial survival skill is the capacity to label our thoughts as 'bad mood thinking'. If we believe our thoughts when sleep deprived, we are on a fast-track to what Buddhists call a hell realm. Develop the reflex of jumping in to cut off the sad stories we have told ourselves so many times, the tales of anger and woundedness.

When sleep deprived we need to make mental health our number one priority. Guard it vigilantly. Nourish it at every opportunity.

See also Fatigue, Sleeplessness

SLEEPLESSNESS

During a group discussion I asked Buddhist teacher Subhana Barzaghi this question: *'The emphasis in Buddhism seems to be in never blocking or ignoring your emotions but rather being with them. I have a tendency to wake up in the dead of night and feel prone to highly irrational anxiety. My preference is to block all thoughts and concentrate on my breath as my best chance of falling back asleep. Is this un-Buddhist?'*

Subhana answered, *'No, not at all. In the Buddhist tradition there are a number of strategies for dealing with difficulties. You don't always have to use the same approach. A useful metaphor is the poison berry tree. One strategy is you cut the tree down and get rid of it—which is what you described doing in bed at night: blocking any troublesome thoughts. A second strategy is that you put up signs around the tree labelling the different berries such as "anger", "fear" or "sadness"—this is the Buddhist technique of allowing your thoughts to proceed and simply noting whatever comes up. The third strategy is to study the tree—the difficult emotion—for it provides the berries to create a medicine for future afflictions. The "medicine" might come for example from clearly seeing what you cling to and how it makes you suffer—and letting go of the causes of suffering.'*

See also Anxiety

STEWING

We sometimes call it 'analysis paralysis': when we have done nothing but stew about a problem yet feel no closer to a breakthrough. While thinking about our difficulties is useful to a point, we tend to take it too far and become obsessive. I believe the Buddha was right in seeing the human race as massively deluded—the way we insist on overlooking the unsatisfactoriness, impermanence and interconnectedness of every person and object. For this reason we need to be very sceptical about the degree to which our thoughts are any reflection of reality.

Creating some spaciousness and tranquillity in our minds can be a large step towards solving a problem. Consider the 'forest pool' metaphor so popular in Buddhism. After inclement weather, the pool is muddy, full of sediment and debris. We cannot clear it by trying to control the contents—that would make the pool worse. We can only wait for all the sediment to settle to the bottom, leaving the pool clear again. So in meditation, by concentrating on our breath or our body or the sounds we can hear in the present moment, we create a space for clarity. We often find that in this spaciousness, an answer to a problem will simply 'pop up' to the surface. Sometimes it won't, but our bodies will thank us for a break from all the worrying.

See also Worrying

STUCKNESS

Some of our domestic hassles with family members seem impossible to solve: the perpetually messy bedroom, the temper outbursts, the sibling bickering or difficult personality traits. I remember a child psychologist addressing a hall of parents, asking: *'What does it take for parents to realise that whatever they're doing isn't working? So often parents tell me: "We've argued about it every day for years," or, "I've told him my opinion a hundred times." Yet still they continue trying to squash a behaviour exactly the same way.'* How easy it is to over-rely on yelling, nagging, threatening or blaming as our reflex parenting technique.

Pema Chödrön, a Canadian teacher in the Tibetan tradition, suggests that in the moment that we notice ourselves falling into a familiar reaction, we pause, and try something new. This is a way to break up stale energy and entrenched thinking patterns. Cognitive behavioural therapy, championed by psychologists, also teaches the value of trying something new in moments when we find ourselves caught in habit. We might, for example, meet our child's misbehaviour with a distraction, a contract, an incentive, a new type of consequence—or even a hug. Last school holidays I found myself reprimanding my sons every few minutes, so I drew up a code of conduct applying to their behaviour, and mine. We negotiated, agreed and signed. It did help.

See also Entrapment

Suppression

In modern Western life, a barrage of advertising teaches us that we need never feel a negative emotion. We can always fix ourselves up with the latest product—with all its added newness. A highly effective way to suppress negative feelings is by using alcohol and other drugs. Recovering addicts sometimes take away from rehab a sheet of paper showing drawings of seventy faces displaying different emotions (frustrated, relieved, exasperated . . .) to help them identify the emotions they have been numbing for years. Even those free of serious addictions can mask their emotions using television, workaholism and other forms of distraction.

Yet we pay a price if we habitually suppress our emotions: we lose self-awareness, we miss opportunities to learn from our feelings and heal ourselves. We also deny ourselves a chance to understand our children's emotions and become more compassionate. The Buddhist approach to coping with the various emotions that arise throughout a day is to practise hospitality. We treat each emotion as a visitor—sure, we may not love this particular visitor, but he won't be here for long so let's see what he has to say. We don't have to obey our visitor or let him lead us astray. We try to be open and tolerant and we learn from him. Vietnamese monk Thich Nhat Hanh suggests we say, for example, *'Hello, Anger. I see you. I accept you.'*

TEENAGE EGOCENTRISM

Professor of child psychology David Elkind describes teenagers' self-absorption as *adolescent egocentrism*. He claims it gives rise to a mental construction he has named *the personal fable*. Each teenager is the main character in their very own personal fable in which they entertain an exaggerated sense of the uniqueness of their feelings and experiences. They say, for example, *Nobody understands me, You just don't know how it feels, Nobody's ever felt love as deeply as ours, You don't know what it feels like to be rejected.*

Some theorists take issue with the personal fable being part of adolescence, arguing it can extend well into young adulthood. Personally, I have seen evidence of the personal fable well before and long after adolescence in the humans around (and including) me, even if it is more pronounced in adolescence. Yet when we finally reach the stage where we can admit that others experience the same intense feelings we do, not only do we feel less isolated but our compassion becomes available for others. The Buddha urged us to contemplate 'the feelings in feelings', which means we allow ourselves to fully experience a feeling without blocking or numbing it. The more we can do this for our own painful emotions, the more we can do it for others.

See also Teenage self-consciousness

TEENAGE
SELF-CONSCIOUSNESS

Part of teenage egocentrism, according to Dr David Elkind, is teenagers' mental construction of an *imaginary audience*. They feel they are always 'on stage' and that everybody notices even their smallest gestures. They are highly sensitive to the potential of others to evaluate them. They feel under scrutiny whenever in public.

As with the teenager's personal fable (*see* Teenage egocentrism), theorists question whether the sense of an imaginary audience is only part of adolescence and whether it does not extend into early adulthood. Again, I see the imaginary audience as a potentially life-long syndrome as we all dedicate untold mental space to the question, 'How do others perceive me?'—even if this question is more preoccupying in the teenage years.

Feeling self-conscious in our interactions with others robs our encounters of joy. It drives many adults to drink their way through every social occasion. One antidote is to become comfortable in our own skin, but this option is not instantly available to all of us. One option that is available to everyone, teenagers and adults alike, is to shift our focus to how others in a social situation might be feeling and to make it our aim to reassure them or put them at ease. The newcomers to a social group, the shy, or socially anxious, those 'outside the clique'—how are they feeling and how could I help them to relax?

See also Teenage egocentrism

127

TEMPTATION

Revenge! Adultery. A binge. Taking what is not given. Giving someone a piece of your mind. Running away. Throttling an obnoxious child. Most of us indulge in fantasies about some of these temptations but sometimes, as we know, fantasy threatens to become reality.

What we need to remember when our defences are low is the Buddha's teaching of karma: *'Wherever we go, wherever we remain, the results of our actions follow us.'* Every action we take, even every thought, has a result—or becomes a contributing condition for what happens next. The Buddha explained what follows our thoughts: *'The thought manifests as the word; the word manifests as the deed; the deed develops into habit; and habit hardens into character.'* With every thought and action we engage in, we reinforce our patterns of behaviour—patterns that can be very hard to undo, and patterns that shape our destiny.

That's why the present moment—the only moment we can control—is so very important. It might be counterproductive to try to suppress tempting fantasies, as they have a way of finding their way to the surface. However, try to be aware of what is really going on when you fantasise. What are some of your beliefs, for example, about what makes you happy? While the Buddhist path is one of awareness, it is undeniably also one of virtue and morality.

See also Immorality

THINKING

Parents have a million things to think about and might welcome the idea of meditation as a chance to take a break from their restless, racing minds. Understanding that thoughts can contribute so much to our stress levels, many Western parents begin to demonise thinking. Yet thinking is what the mind does and most of us cannot stop it for long. Western meditators can spend their whole sitting—or a whole Buddhist retreat—engaged in a war against thoughts. They usually lose the battle and develop a sense of failure about their meditation abilities. Still more Westerners never even try meditation, seeing themselves as incapable of meditating altogether, simply because they cannot 'stop' their thoughts.

The wisest Buddhist teachers have diagnosed these tendencies to beat ourselves up for thinking and advise us to foster an attitude of 'allowing'. Allow thoughts to arise and watch them. We practise equanimity by trying not to become too entangled and lost in them, but when we do, we simply notice that and sharpen our awareness. Zen Buddhists call this 'just sitting'. With no specific meditation object we are aware of whatever arises and passes away in the present moment, be it bodily sensations, emotions or thoughts. We need to be aware of our thoughts—their contents, consequences and truthfulness—not eradicate them.

TIME-WASTING

As busy as we are, many parents feel frustrated with their own time-wasting. The methods of time-wasting are different for everyone and might include watching too much poor-quality television, reading trashy magazines, endlessly surfing the net or playing computer games. The Buddha would often mention the wastefulness of 'idle chatter' where we gossip, whinge or prattle away about nothing, with little concern for the listener. Our children too are in danger of wasting vast swathes of their childhood if we never intercept the influences of popular culture.

It helps to remember that our lives are extremely short and that death is the only certainty. Only with a deep understanding of this fact will we ever understand that every moment is precious. Every moment is a gift. If we need to relax and unwind, we can do it in a way that truly nourishes us: turn off the radio and soak up the present, mute the television advertisements and talk to your loved ones, drop the celebrity gossip magazine and read something inspiring. See your mind—and each of your children's minds—as a muscle. It needs to work out and it needs deep rest. In the words of the poet Mary Oliver, who is often quoted by Buddhist teachers, *Tell me, what is it you plan to do with your one wild and precious life?*

TODDLER TANTRUMS

The most important message to convey to a tantrumming toddler is that their behaviour does not achieve the results they desire. The results a toddler desires might not be solely a specific outcome, but might also be attention or the drama of a fight with a parent. This means that our focus as parents is to avoid becoming emotionally entangled in the scene. When we shout, argue or smack, we fuel it. The challenge is to rise above the scene, to achieve a sense of perspective. As all-consuming as a toddler's tantrum can feel to us emotionally, we can soothe ourselves with those timeless Buddhist words, *'This too will pass.'* Just as a particular tantrum will pass, so too will the whole toddler tantrum stage.

A toddler tantrum is an opportunity to practise patience, the opposite of anger and, according to Buddhism, one of the most important qualities. The sensations of the breath and the body are available in the present and by focusing on them we not only calm ourselves but slow the negative thoughts that might arise; thoughts that only exaggerate the harm (*This is unbearable*), pretend the situation is permanent (*This will never end*), and make the episode personal (*I'm such an ineffective parent*). If such thoughts do arise, we just watch them and realise we do not need to believe them.

See also Compartmentalising, Seriousness

131

TOO MUCH TECHNOLOGY

One of the greatest gifts we can give our children is the opportunity to enjoy nature. It is a worry in this technological age that many children might miss out on the chance to learn the power of nature to comfort us, relax us and shift our perspective on our cares and concerns. In the bush, at the beach or in the local park, our capacity to be calm, open and present multiplies. Addicted to the adrenaline of computer games or the distractions of television, some children see no need to step outside. I have taken friends of my sons on bushwalks only to hear them complain they feel scared—so unfamiliar was the experience.

In nature we experience a simple and accessible form of happiness. In the outdoors children are active, creative and keen to explore. Outside, they are free to be children, to enjoy an active childhood and to create the very best of memories. As parents we can model passion for nature, pointing out its wonders—and children invariably return the favour. If our children do not learn to love nature, how can we trust future generations to preserve it?

See also Overstimulation

TRYING TOO HARD

An important factor of the Buddha's Noble Eightfold Path is Skilful Effort. We usually define this as a middle road between being a fierce dharma warrior (battling greed, hatred and delusion) and a lazy hippie. It is worth remaining mindful of our own level of effort when it comes to parenting, working and practising Buddhist teachings, for extremes can be perilous.

When caught up in what Buddhists call '*efforting*', we find ourselves grim-faced and tense in our daily duties—or in our approach to practice—obsessed with 'getting it done' or 'getting it right'. Here is an ancient story from the Tao:

'Prince Wen Hui praised the faultless method of his cook in cutting up an ox. The cook thanked the prince and explained how he had managed to retain a perfectly sharp knife for nineteen years. Rather than looking on the ox as a mass to hack through, the cook opened himself every time to the natural line of the bones, alive to the secret openings and hidden spaces of the joints. Moving slowly, watching closely, the cook slid his knife effortlessly through the meat and allowed the joy of the work to sink in.'

Our own tasks too, can be more flowing, less effortful, when we pause and make space for a quiet intimacy with the experience.

See also Carnivorousness, Expectations of ourselves,
Guilt, Lobotomies

UNCONSCIOUSNESS

We may remember our pre-parenting years as a time of seeking pleasure and avoiding pain. When we become parents, most of us realise there is more to life than hedonism, and our daily goals become more sophisticated and more focused on others, particularly our children. In times of boredom it is easy to revert to that old model of ourselves as pleasure-seekers as we feel a need for something extreme to wake us up: an alcoholic binge, a culinary treat, a luxury holiday, an affair, some kind of thrill. This is usually a sign we are living without awareness, that we have lost our capacity for absorbing simple wonders.

Living on automatic, failing to notice both our surroundings and our inner world, we find ourselves feeling dull, lethargic and restless. Some of us develop a habit of blocking strong feelings so that all we feel is numb. What can one do when life lacks texture, taste and joy? A Zen Buddhist might suggest adopting a 'beginner's mind', where we meet each new moment with the fresh eyes of someone who has dropped in for the first time. We suspend our tired old biases and judgements and gaze with wonder, listen with openness, rally all our senses for a full experience of the moment. This is especially worthwhile in the presence of our children, who can intrigue and delight us far more often than we let them.

See also Boredom

UNEMPLOYMENT

Now that the 'global financial crisis' has come and gone I am running out of friends who can say they have never experienced unemployment. A state we may have worried about and feared for many years, when unemployment finally strikes, our mental health can come under siege. Job hunting is an emotional rollercoaster ride of raised hopes and disappointments. Our minds know no end of worrying about what the future might hold: losing our home? Changing our children's school? Downsizing our lifestyle?

One of the greatest challenges unemployment poses is to our identity. For most of us, our job contributes enormously to our sense of who we are. 'What do you do?' is invariably one of our first questions on meeting someone new. Buddhist teachings inform us, however, that seeing our job—or any role we play, be it worker, parent or volunteer—as our identity limits us immensely. With our essential Buddha nature, we are beings with an infinite capacity to love others, act courageously and contribute to the world. Feeling at a loose end, without a specific role to play, we might feel lost and insecure in the first weeks of unemployment, but many then discover other ways to give that enrich their families, friends and communities.

You are not your job. You are not a role. Why limit your identity?

See also Rejection

WORRYING

Giving ourselves over to worrying is dangerous for our karma: the more we worry, the more we worry. That is, through allowing worry to become a habit we condition ourselves into characters more inclined to worrying.

In my own family, my very loving grandmother was a dreadful worrier and the result was that nobody told her anything. For parents to remain approachable, their children—particularly older ones—need to know their parents can cope with the necessary risks they take as well as the inevitability that, to some degree, they will suffer. The problem with worrying is that it forces us to live in an imaginary, non-existent future and denies us the opportunity to live mindfully in the present. Moreover, it is often a complete waste of time. As French Renaissance writer Michel de Montaigne said, *'My life has been full of terrible misfortunes, most of which never happened.'*

Psychologists have found that even when what we worry about does come to pass, we find the event less painful than expected, for most of us are highly capable of drawing on our inner resources. When you catch yourself worrying way past the point where you can help anyone, label your thoughts 'inappropriate attention'. This is a common label in Buddhist circles that serves as a red stop sign.

See also Anxiety, Fear, Stewing

YEARNING

Self-employed, I long for prospective clients to call me—but also worry that a new client will be too time-consuming. I long to hear from friends, but at the same time for the peacefulness of solitude. One of the reasons the Buddha taught that our desires cause us to suffer is that they are often contradictory, and this confuses and exhausts us. Sitting in meditation, or just being mindful throughout our day, we also notice that desires—or self-centred cravings—constantly proliferate. They arise inexhaustibly, turning us all into what Buddhists call 'hungry ghosts' with wide-open mouths that can never be filled. Parents have all their desires for their own lives but also many hundred for their children's lives. We want them to score goals, win prizes, avoid disappointments and behave well.

If we take all these desires seriously they will run us ragged. Yet most of us treat them like orders: *I must have this now* or, *I must be free of that now*. The Buddha encourages us to develop an awareness of the manic nature of our desires by observing them throughout our day, or ideally throughout a meditation sitting. We can label them as they arise, *Oh, another desire arising*. This allows us to take a step back from the desire and become less entangled by it. When we see clearly we can even *let go* of a desire and taste some freedom. Our desires quieten down when we practise gratitude for what we have and if we cultivate inner peace and contentment.

ACKNOWLEDGEMENTS

Firstly, I need to thank the widely loved Ajahn Brahm from Perth, Australia, for allowing me to quote two wonderful stories from his vast personal collection. The Venerable Thubten Chodron from the United States was also generous with her time and insights on the topic of guilt. The teachers at my *sangha* inspire my daily practice and include Jason Siff and Stephen and Martine Batchelor when they visit Australia, Winton Higgins, Patrick Kearney, Chris McLean, Joyce Kornblatt, Victor von der Heyde, Venerable Sujato and Michael Dash. Teacher Subhana Barzaghi has been generous and supportive in her contributions to all my books and is a vast reservoir of *dharma* experience. Jonathan Page chairs my *sangha* and has a spiritual practice that never fails to inspire. My friend Anna Street, a mother from my *sangha*, is endlessly encouraging, enthusiastic and wise. Thanks also to my family and my friends and to Allen & Unwin.

BIBLIOGRAPHY

Agassi, Andre, *Open: An autobiography*, HarperCollins, London, 2009, pp. 186–7

Commonwealth of Australia, *Talking with Your Kids about Drugs*, AGPS, Canberra, August 2007

Dalai Lama, His Holiness the, *The Art of Happiness: A handbook for living*, Hodder, Sydney, 1998, pp. 68–9

Elkind, David, 'Egocentrism in adolescence', *Child Development*, 1967, no. 38, pp. 1025–34

Ferrucci, Piero, *The Gifts of Parenting: Learning and growing with our children*, Pan Macmillan, Sydney, 1999, p. 11

Joko Beck, Charlotte, *Nothing Special: Living Zen*, HarperCollins, New York, 1993, pp. 232–3

Maezen Miller, Karen, *Momma Zen: Walking the crooked path of mother-hood*, Trumpeter, Boston, 2006, pp. 54, 100

Magid, Barry, 'Five practices to change you', *Tricycle: The Buddhist review*, Summer 2005, p. 39

Oliver, Mary, 'The Summer Day', *New and Selected Poems*, Beacon Press, Boston, 1992

Patty, Anna, 'Helicopter parents not doing enough to let children fail', *Sydney Morning Herald*, 2 April 2010

Peck, M. Scott, *The Road Less Travelled: A new psychology of love, traditional values and spiritual growth*, Simon & Schuster, New York, 1978

Singer, Peter, *Animal Liberation: A new ethics for our treatment of animals*, Random House, New York, 1975

Spock, Benjamin, and Parker, Stephen J., *Dr Spock's Baby and Child Care*, Pocket Books, New York, 1992, pp. xxvii, 1

'Napthali's book focuses on Buddhist practices that will help mothers become calmer and happier in themselves. Follow her advice and we all know what comes next—better parenting.'—*Sunday Telegraph*

'Funny, uplifting, reassuring, real and wise. A truly "mothering" book for mothers.'—Stephanie Dowrick

'This is an excellent, practical guide to everyday Buddhism, not just for mothers, but for everyone who has ever had a mother.'—Vicki Mackenzie, author of the best-selling *Why Buddhism?*

'If you liked her first book, *Buddhism for Mothers*, then you'll adore this one. It'll give you a new perspective on parenting and may even help you enjoy it more.'—*Sunday Telegraph*

'This second book from Sarah Napthali . . . had me repeatedly crying out "yes" . . . By being focused, open and more attentive to the present moment we can enjoy a calmer and happier journey through parenthood; a great companion book for mothers struggling to cope with their new role.'—*Perth Woman*

'Sarah Napthali's terrific first book *Buddhism for Mothers* showed new mothers how to be calm and contented in the face of the radical shift in their lives. Now Napthali tweaks her Buddhist theories to suit mothers of school-aged children who might be finding that the busy lives of children are taking everyone away from the core values that lead to a fulfilled life.'—*Sunday Mail*